Drums

US Level 2 (UK Grade 2)

Performance pieces, technical exercises and in-depth guidance for Rockschool assessments

ISBN 978-1-78936-158-2

Visit Hal Leonard Online at
www.halleonard.com

World headquarters, contact:
Hal Leonard
7777 West Bluemound Road
Milwaukee, WI 53213
Email: info@halleonard.com

In Europe, contact:
Hal Leonard Europe Limited
1 Red Place
London, W1K 6PL
Email: info@halleonardeurope.com

In Australia, contact:
Hal Leonard Australia Pty. Ltd.
4 Lentara Court
Cheltenham, Victoria, 3192 Australia
Email: info@halleonard.com.au

Acknowledgements

Catalogue Number: RSK200062US
ISBN: 978-1-78936-158-2
Initial US Release | Errata details can be found at *www.rslawards.com/errata*

CONTACTING ROCKSCHOOL
www.rslawards.com
Telephone: +44 (0)345 460 4747
Email: *info@rslawards.com*

Syllabus Designer
Nik Preston

Producer
Nik Preston

Syllabus Advisor and Project Management
Sharon Kelly

Proof reading
Sharon Kelly, Jono Harrison, Nik Preston (and all arrangers/performers)

Syllabus Consultants (Hit Tunes 2018 Repertoire)
Guitar: James Betteridge, Andy G Jones
Bass: Joe Hubbard, Diego Kovadloff, Joel McIver
Drums: Paul Elliott, Pete Riley

Arrangers (Hit Tunes 2018 Repertoire)
Guitar: James Betteridge, Andy G Jones, Mike Goodman, Viv Lock
Bass: Diego Kovadloff, Andy Robertson, Joe Hubbard
Drums: Paul Elliott, Stu Roberts, Pete Riley

Publishing (Hit Tunes 2018 Repertoire)
Fact files by Diego Kovadloff
Covers designed by Phil Millard (Rather Nice design)
Music engraving, internal design and layout by
Simon Troup & Jennie Troup (Digital Music Art)

Distribution
Exclusive Distributors: Hal Leonard

Musicians (Hit Tunes 2018 Repertoire)
Guitar: Andy G Jones, James Betteridge, Mike Goodman, David Rhodes (Peter Gabriel)
Bass: Nik Preston, Joe Hubbard, Stuart Clayton, Andy Robertson, John Illsley (Dire Straits)
Drums: Paul Elliott, Pete Riley, Peter Huntington, Stu Roberts, Billy Cobham (Miles Davis, Mahavishnu Orchestra)
Vocals: Kim Chandler
Keys: Jono Harrison, Hannah V (on 'Red Baron'), Andy Robertson
Horns: Tom Walsh (tpt), Martin Williams (sax), Andy Wood (trmb)

Endorsements (Hit Tunes 2018 Repertoire)
Nik Preston: Overwater basses, Positive Grid amps
Paul Elliott: Liberty drums, Istanbul Mehmet cymbals, Regal Tip drumsticks, Remo heads, ACS custom ear plugs, Protection Racket cases
Stu Roberts: Paiste cymbals, Regal Tip drumsticks, Yamaha drums, Protection Racket cases

Recording & Audio Engineering (Hit Tunes 2018 Repertoire)
Recording engineers: Oli Jacobs, Scott Barnett, Patrick Phillips
Mixing engineer: Samuel Vasanth
Mastering engineer: Samuel Vasanth
Audio production: Nik Preston
Audio management: Ash Preston, Samuel Vasanth
Recording studios: Real World Studios, The Premises

Publishing (Rockschool 2012 Repertoire)
Fact Files written by Joe Bennett, Charlie Griffiths, Stephen Lawson, Simon Pitt, Stuart Ryan and James Uings
Walkthroughs written by James Uings
Music engraving, internal design and layout by
Simon Troup & Jennie Troup (Digital Music Art)
Proof reading and copy editing by Chris Bird, Claire Davies, Stephen Lawson, Simon Pitt and James Uings
Publishing administration by Caroline Uings
Additional drum proof reading by Miguel Andrews

Instrumental Specialists (Rockschool 2012 Repertoire)
Guitar: James Uings
Bass: Stuart Clayton
Drums: Noam Lederman

Musicians (Rockschool 2012 Repertoire)
Andy Crompton, Camilo Tirado, Carl Sterling, Charlie Griffiths, Chris Webster, Dave Marks, DJ Harry Love, Felipe Karam, Fergus Gerrand, Henry Thomas, Jake Painter, James Arben, James Uings, Jason Bowld, Joe Bennett, Jon Musgrave, Kishon Khan, Kit Morgan, Larry Carlton, Neel Dhorajiwala, Nir Z, Noam Lederman, Norton York, Richard Pardy, Ross Stanley, Simon Troup, Steve Walker, Stuart Clayton, Stuart Ryan

Endorsements (Rockschool 2012 Repertoire)
Noam Lederman: Mapex drums, Paiste cymbals, Vic Firth Sticks

Recording & Audio Engineering (Rockschool 2012 Repertoire)
Recorded at The Farm (Fisher Lane Studios)
Produced and engineered by Nick Davis
Assistant engineer and Pro Tools operator Mark Binge
Mixed and mastered at Langlei Studios
Mixing and additional editing by Duncan Jordan
Supporting Tests recorded by Duncan Jordan and Kit Morgan
Mastered by Duncan Jordan
Executive producers: James Uings, Jeremy Ward and Noam Lederman

Executive Producers
John Simpson, Norton York

Table of Contents

Introductions & Information

Hit Tunes

Rockschool Originals

Technical Exercises

Supporting Tests

Additional Information

Welcome to Rockschool Drums Level/Grade 2

Welcome to Drums Level/Grade 2

Welcome to the **Rockschool 2018 Drums syllabus**. This book and the accompanying downloadable audio contain everything you need to play drums at this level/grade. In the book you will find the assessment scores in standard drum notation, as well as Fact Files and Walkthroughs for each song.

The downloadable audio includes:

- full stereo mixes of six Rockschool compositions and six arrangements of classic and contemporary hits
- backing tracks (in both click and no-click versions, minus the assessed drum part)
- all necessary audio for the complete range of supporting tests

Drum Assessments

At each level/grade, you have the option of taking one of two different types of assessment:

- **Level/Grade Assessment:** a Level/Grade Assessment is a mixture of music performances, technical work and tests. You prepare three pieces (two of which may be Free Choice Pieces) and the contents of the Technical Exercise section. This accounts for 75% of the assessment marks. The other 25% consists of: ***either*** a Sight Reading ***or*** an Improvisation & Interpretation test (10%), a pair of instrument specific Ear Tests (10%) and finally you will be asked five General Musicianship Questions (5%). The pass mark is 60%.

- **Performance Certificate:** in a Performance Certificate you play five pieces. Up to three of these can be Free Choice Pieces. Each song is marked out of 20 and the pass mark is 60%.

Book Contents

The book is divided into a number of sections. These are:

- **Assessment Pieces:** in this book you will find six specially commissioned pieces of Level/Grade 2 standard. Each of these is preceded by a ***Fact File***. Each Fact File contains a summary of the song, its style, tempo, key and technical features, along with a list of the musicians who played on it. The song itself is printed on two pages. Immediately after each song is a ***Walkthrough***. This covers the song from a performance perspective, focusing on the technical issues you will encounter. Each song comes with a full mix version and a backing track. Both versions have spoken count-ins at the beginning. Please note that any solos played on the full mix versions are indicative only.

- **Technical Exercises:** You should prepare the exercises set in this level/grade as indicated. There is also a Fill test which should be practised and played to the backing track.

- **Supporting Tests and General Musicianship Questions:** in Drums Level/Grade 2 there are three supporting tests – ***either*** a Sight Reading ***or*** an Improvisation & Interpretation test and two Ear Tests – and a set of General Musicianship Questions (GMQs) asked at the end of each assessment. Examples of the types of tests likely to appear in the assessment are printed in this book. Additional examples of both types of test and the GMQs can be found in the Rockschool *Companion Guide To Drums.*

- **Additional Information:** finally, you will find information on assessment procedures and marking schemes.

Audio

Audio is provided in the form of backing tracks (minus drums, and in two versions: click and no-click) and examples (including drums) for the pieces and the supporting tests where applicable. Audio files are supplied in MP3 format to enable playback on a wide range of compatible devices. Digital versions of the book include audio files in the download. Download audio for hardcopy books from RSL directly at *www.rslawards.com/downloads* — you will need to input this code when prompted: **TPCG4QT98E**

Syllabus Guide

All candidates should read the accompanying syllabus guide when using this level/grade book. This can be downloaded from the RSL website: *www.rslawards.com*

Errata

Updates and changes to Rockschool books are documented online. Candidates should check for errata periodically while studying for any assessment. Further details can be found on the RSL website: *www.rslawards.com/errata*

SONG TITLE: LOSING MY RELIGION
ALBUM: OUT OF TIME
LABEL: WARNER BROS.
GENRE: ALTERNATIVE ROCK / FOLK ROCK / POP ROCK

WRITTEN BY: BILL BERRY, PETER BUCK, MIKE MILLS AND MICHAEL STIPE
PRODUCED BY: SCOTT LITT AND R.E.M

US CHART PEAK: 4

BACKGROUND INFO

'Losing My Religion' was the first single from R.E.M's 1991 album *Out Of Time*. The song reached the no. 4 spot on the Billboard Hot 100 chart and pushed the band into the mainstream. *Out Of Time* received seven Grammy Award nominations and won three, including Best Alternative Music Album.

The song originated from a Mandolin line guitarist Peter Buck developed through practising. He had recently started to play the instrument and used to record himself to analyse his practice. Upon listening back to one of those recordings, he stumbled across the line and the song was built from there. The song is built around a generic chord sequence that is pushed along by a Fleetwood Mac-esque bass line, simple but solid drums, and an acoustic guitar played by the band's touring guitarist Peter Holsapple holding the song together on the midrange. Lead singer Michael Stipe delivers the song with poignancy and in a loose and straightforward fashion. The song is about romantic expression and unrequited love. The expression 'losing my religion' is used in the Southern United States and it means losing one's temper or being at the end of one's rope. Michael Stipe has compared the song's theme of obsession and love to The Police's 'Every Breath You Take'. Another link between the two bands is that in 1980 R.E.M were signed to I.R.S, a subsidiary of A&M Records, founded by Miles Copeland, The Police's manager. *Out Of Time* sold nearly ten million copies worldwide. The band is accompanied by a string section from the Atlanta Symphony Orchestra.

Drummer Bill Berry is a multi-instrumentalist who also played guitar, bass and piano and wrote songs for the band. His drumming style is simple and complimentary with a strong backbeat. He left the band in 1997, after seventeen years, following an on-stage collapse during a show in Lausanne, Switzerland. He recovered and re-joined the band but, after reconsidering, he decided that he did not have the drive to continue with the lifestyle required by R.E.M's touring schedule. The band respected his decision and continued as a trio with drummers Joey Waronker and Bill Rieflin taking the drum seat. Berry left the music business and became a hay farmer in Farmington, near Athens, Georgia. He performed again with R.E.M when they were inducted into the Rock and Roll Hall of Fame.

Losing My Religion

REM
Words & Music by Peter Buck,
Michael Mills, Michael Stipe & William Berry

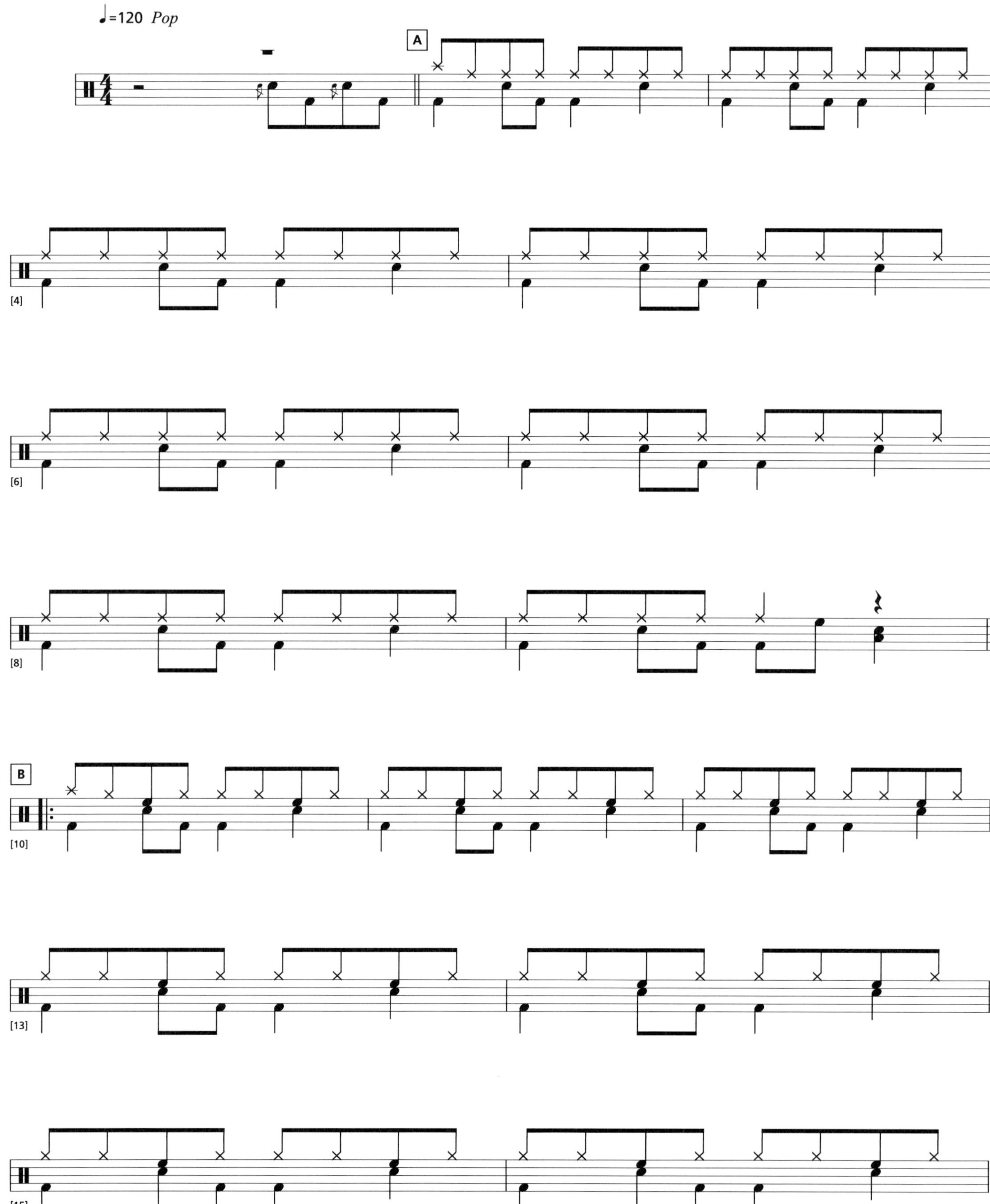

1.
2.
[17]
C
[19]
[21]
[23]
[25]
D
[27]
[29]

Walkthrough

Pick Up and A Section (Measures 1–9)

This pop track comes in with a half measure 'pick up' fill, which complements the melodic riff. The pattern is played through eighth notes and provides quite an energetic and powerful opening to the track, due to the sonic combination of snare drum flams and bass drum.

The flams should be played with power and definition. Be positive and play each note of the flam at the same volume – commonly known as a power flam.

To lock in with the track, it's always advisable to internalise the subdivisional time-feel before coming in with the drums, particularly considering the half measure 'pick up'. Given the tempo, it's best to feel and count eighth notes (1 & 2 & 3 & 4 &), which will help with the timing and consistency of the groove throughout the track.

Following the 'pick up', the A Section settles into an eighth note groove played on the ride cymbal, with snare drum backbeats and a repetitive bass drum pattern. At measure 9 there is a fill on high tom on the '&' of beat 3, followed by a unison between snare drum and floor tom on beat 4, which sets the scene for the B section.

For general guidance on the structure and feel of the groove throughout the whole arrangement, pay attention to co-ordination and related unisons between hi-hat, bass drum and snare drum. Unisons should fall together, so be careful not to flam. Focus on the dynamic balance and consistency of sounds within the groove. Listen to how the groove locks in with the backing track. How does it sound? Is it consistent?

Given the tempo and feel of this track, playing accents on the hi-hat or ride cymbal is a great way to enhance the feel of the groove. This is a very common technique, which incorporates the use of specific strokes – known as down strokes and up strokes. In a typical eighth note groove application, the down stroke provides the accent on the downbeat and the up stroke plays quieter on the offbeat.

B Section (Measures 10–18)

This section features a predominant eighth note groove on the hi-hat, together with snare backbeats played in unison with the tom and bass drum variations. Be careful not to flam on the snare and tom unison. Notice the repeats at measure 10, together with first and second time endings at measures 17 and 18, respectively. Watch out for the fill at the end of measure 18, which finishes on the floor tom and moves to the crash cymbal to begin the C Section.

C Section (Measures 19–26)

Be sure to anticipate the movement of the eighth notes from the hi-hat in the previous section to the crash at measure 19, then to the ride cymbal for the remainder of this section. The groove in this section is essentially repetitive, though punctuated by short fills at the end of measures 20, 22, 24 and 26.

D Section (Measures 27–30)

These final four measures have a spacious feel, and feature eighth notes on the hi hat with unison bass drum on the first and last notes of each measure – together with open and closed hi-hat figures. Be positive and make a good connection with the stick when opening and closing the hi-hat cymbals. The track ends with a crash cymbal and bass drum unison on beat 1 of measure 30.

Marvin Gaye

SONG TITLE: I HEARD IT THROUGH THE GRAPEVINE
ALBUM: IN THE GROOVE
LABEL: TAMLA
GENRE: R&B / PSYCHEDELIC SOUL

WRITTEN BY: NORMAN WHITFIELD AND BARRETT STRONG
PRODUCED BY: NORMAN WHITFIELD

US CHART PEAK: 1

BACKGROUND INFO

'I Heard It Through The Grapevine' was written by Motown's songwriter and producer Norman Whitfield and first recorded by The Miracles in 1966.

Marvin Gaye recorded the song in 1967. His version took over a month to complete because Whitfield was experimenting with overdubs of Gaye's vocal and The Andante's backing vocals as well as mixing several rhythm tracks cut by The Funk Brothers. Whitfield also added strings recorded by the Detroit Symphony Orchestra and arranged by Paul Riser. Gaye and Whitfield had a number of arguments during the recording because Whitfield wanted Gaye to sing in a key that pushed him out of his comfortable range, such as he did with David Ruffin when recording 'Ain't Too Proud To Beg' with The Temptations, a trick that worked to great effect. The song ended up sounding as Whitfield desired and was approved by the Quality Control department. Berry Gordy, however, blocked its release as a single.

Later in 1967 Whitfield re-arranged the song to be recorded by Gladys Knight & The Pips. After hearing Aretha Franklin's version of 'Respect', Whitfield added funk elements in keeping with the Muscle Shoals rhythm section in an attempt to 'out-funk' Aretha. Gladys Knight, Bubba Knight, William Guest and Edward Patten worked for several weeks on their vocal arrangement. The single was released, and although it had little backing from Motown, it reached the no. 1 spot on the R&B charts and eventually the no. 2 spot on the Billboard Pop Singles chart. It became Motown's highest selling single at the time. Berry Gordy decided to include it on Gladys Knight's forthcoming album *Everybody Needs Love.*

Despite Whitfield's insistence that Marvin Gaye's version should be released as a single, Gordy only authorised its release as part of the album *In The Groove*. Gaye's version of *I Heard It Through The Grapevine* received so much airplay that Gordy eventually released it as a single, topping the Billboard Pop Singles Chart. *In The Groove* was subsequently re-released as *I Heard It Through The Grapevine*. The success of Gaye's version was not well received by Gladys Knight and this led to a rift between them.

Due to the overdubs used by Whitfield on the recording of Marvin Gaye's version, two drummers from the legendary Funk Brothers (Uriel Jones and Richard Allen) can be heard on the recording.

I Heard It Through The Grapevine

Marvin Gaye

Words & Music by Norman Whitfield & Barrett Strong

Chorus
[17]
cont. sim.
[19]
[21]
[23]
Intro Vamp
[25]
p
[27]
Instrumental Section
[29]
f
[31]

Walkthrough

Intro (Measures 1–4)

The piece begins with the drums playing a pattern with the feet only. The dynamic is 'piano' (soft), so this should be played fairly quietly, possibly using heel-down technique if comfortable. The pattern is the same as that which would normally be played behind a Brazilian samba rhythm, and this kind of repeating pattern is often called an ostinato.

After three measures we have a fill played from high-tom to snare to low-tom. A suitable way to play this would be to keep the right hand playing all of the eighth-notes while the left fills in the last 16th note of the beat 3.

Verse (Measures 5–16)

At measure 5 we encounter the main groove of the piece, where the right hand is playing eighth-notes on the low-tom whilst the left plays 'two' and 'four' on the snare. This is all played over our foot ostinato, which might seem like a lot to get to grips with at first. However, notice that the left hand and left foot are both playing on beats 2 and 4, so it's really only the coordination between the right hand and foot that holds the challenge. In terms of development it would might be easiest to begin with the foot pattern, then add the right hand and introduce the left hand afterwards. Finally, notice that there is no crash on the downbeat of measure 5 and the dynamics have moved from 'piano' to 'forte' (loud).

Measure 16

The verse is 12 measures long and ends with a variation on the basic groove, which works as a simple fill to introduce the chorus. Essentially the left hand plays the last three eighth-notes of the measure, but notice also that the bass drum misses its usual final eighth-note.

Chorus (Measures 17–24)

The chorus is eight measures long and begins in measure 17. The groove is the same as that of the verse, but notice on beat 1 of measure 17 that there is a crash – the right hand will move from the low-tom to play this.

Measure 24

It combines two elements seen so far – the verse groove (on beats 1 and 2) and the fill we saw in measure 4 played here across beats 3 and 4. Again, the easiest way of negotiating this would be to move the right hand from the low-tom on the '&' of beat 2 to the high-tom on beat 3.

Intro Vamp (Measures 25–28)

Measure 25 sees a return to the Intro's foot ostinato and our original quieter dynamic ('piano'). Notice the crash on beat 1 of measure 25 which, in conjunction with the fill in measure 24, probably makes this transition one of the most challenging elements of the piece and one that's probably worth practising as a two-measure cycle. This four-measure section ends with the same fill we saw in the Intro and in measure 4.

Instrumental Section (Measures 29–33)

Measure 29 sees a shift back to our 'forte' dynamic, but also a different groove to those seen so far. We're now playing time on the hi-hats but with a different bass drum pattern. This is another challenging transition – the fill in measure 28 and the new groove and dynamic in measure 29 gives us a lot to negotiate in the space of two measures. The piece ends with an anticipated crash, often referred to as a 'push', on the last eighth-note of measure 32.

SONG TITLE: PASSIONFRUIT
ALBUM: MORE LIFE
LABEL: OVO SOUND / CAH MONEY / YOUNG MONEY
GENRE: ALTERNATIVE ROCK / FOLK ROCK / POP ROCK

WRITTEN BY: AUBREY GRAHAM AND NANA ROGUES
PRODUCED BY: NANA ROGUES

US CHART PEAK: 8

BACKGROUND INFO

'Passionfruit' was released digitally in March 2017 and topped the charts in many countries, as well as reaching no. 8 on the Billboard Hot 100 in the US. The song was co-written by Drake and British producer Nana Rogues. 'Passionfruit' blends Dancehall, R&B, and Pop, and is included on *More Life*, Drake's seventh consecutive no. 1 album.

Drake holds the record for most songs in the Billboard Charts, with 154 entries, 24 Hot 100 songs charted in a single week, and the longest stay in the Hot 100 (431 weeks). In addition, he has multiple streaming accolades and won three Grammy Awards. Prior to his massive success as a hip hop star and producer he was a well known face on the TV teen drama *Degrassi: The Next Generation*. Drake released his debut album *Thank Me Later* in 2010, which reached the no.1 spot on the Billboard 200 charts, and has not stopped since.

Drake was born in October 1986 in Toronto, Canada. His father worked as a drummer and played with Jerry Lee Lewis. His uncle is bassist Larry Graham, of Sly and the Family Stone and Graham Central Station fame, and another paternal uncle was songwriter Teenie Hodges. His father's side of the family are practicing Catholics whereas his mother's are of Jewish Ashkenazi descent. Drake attended a Jewish day school and celebrated his Bar Mitzvah. His parents divorced when he was five and a young Drake witnessed the arrest of his father whilst visiting him in Memphis, Tennessee. He later experienced bullying at school due to his social and religious background. These experiences contributed to forming a world view that is reflected in his early lyrics and made his rapping a matter of much discussion and controversy. He is credited with developing the style known as 'hyper-reality rap' where celebrity related issues, as distinct from 'real world' issues, are focused upon. His rapping style is dexterous and incorporates the singing of melodic passages, something Drake credits his father for.

Drake's live drummer is Adrian Bent. He has also worked with Eminem, Lil Wayne, and Jay-Z and is known for his impeccable technique and powerful groove. Like many of today's hip hop drummers he started young playing in church – so he is well-versed in gospel music and the high technical demands of the style.

Passionfruit

Drake
Words & Music by Noah Shebib,
Nana Bediako Rogues & Audrey Graham

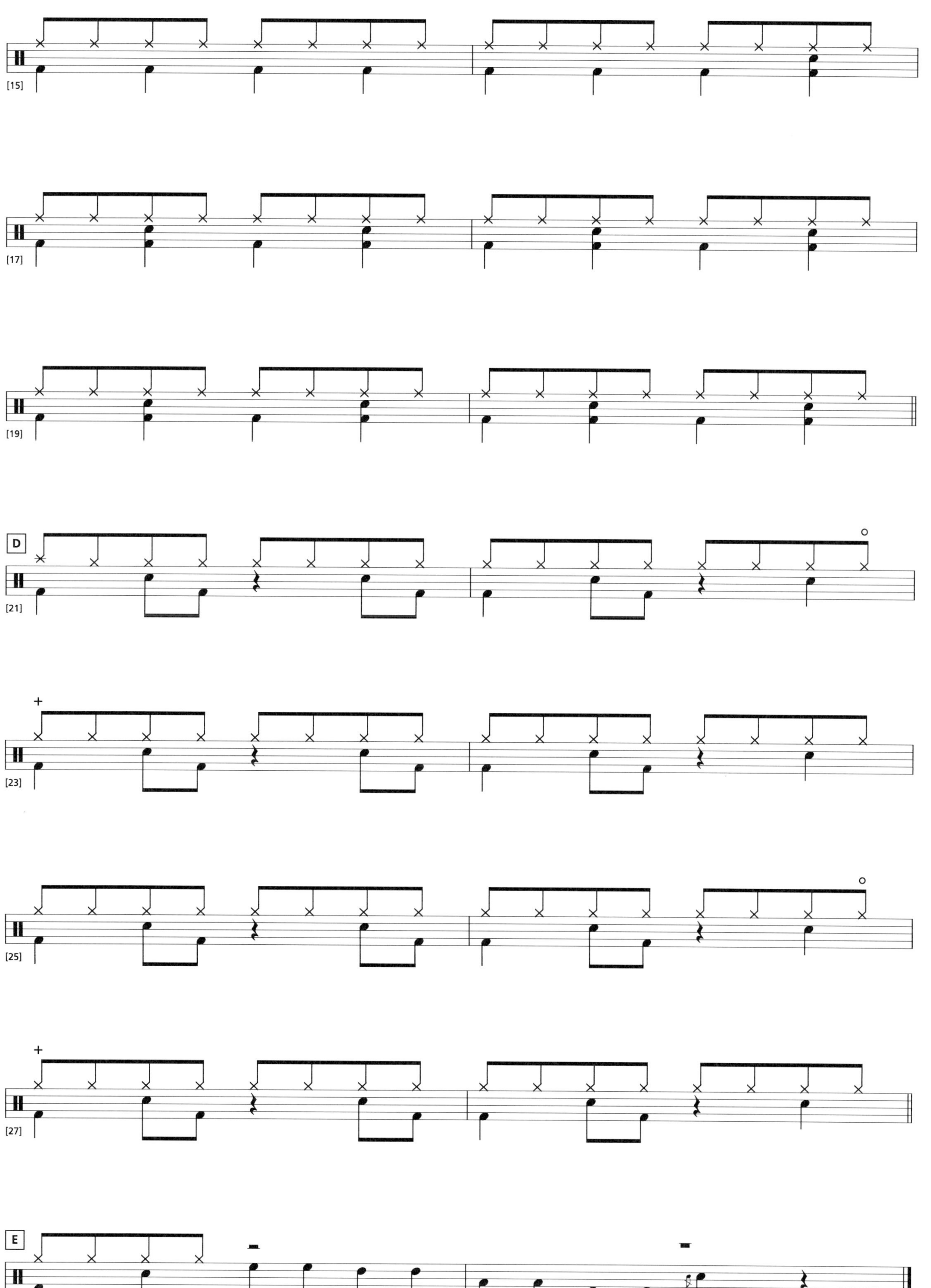
[15]
[17]
[19]
D
[21]
[23]
[25]
[27]
E
[29]

Walkthrough

A Section (Measures 1–4)

This hip hop track begins with a four-measure introduction, featuring a spacious hi-hat and bass drum groove, with the hi-hat playing on offbeat eighth notes and the bass drum playing on beats 1 and 3.

This introduction groove is not particularly technically challenging but playing offbeat eighth notes can be tricky and, in order to lock in with the time-feel of the track, it's important to feel the quarter note pulse and the eighth notes (counted as 1 & 2 & 3 & 4 &) before the drums come in (and then throughout the track). This will help to internalise and develop the timing, feel and consistency of the groove.

B Section (Measures 5–12)

This section features an eighth note groove between hi-hat, snare and bass drum. Aim for a good consistent flow of eighth notes on the hi-hat throughout this section and pay attention to the co-ordination of the bass drum variations and snare drum backbeats – all of which fall in unison with the hi-hat. Those unisons should fall together so be careful not to flam.

Notice the open hi-hats at the end of measure 7. Be positive and make a good connection with the stick when opening and closing the hi-hat cymbals and remember to give the open hi-hat note its full duration, closing on the first note of measure 8. Also, be sure to keep the foot in contact with the pedal board, so as not to lose control and always remain dynamically sensitive to the groove and track.

Be aware of the eighth note unison between hi-hat and snare drum at the end of measure 8 and also the unison figure between hi-hat, snare drum and bass drum over beats 1 and 2 of measure 12.

This figure is followed by a single flam on beat 3. Be positive and play each note of the flam at the same volume – not as a traditional military flam, which would typically have a quieter grace note played before the main note. Playing each note of the flam at the same volume, (most typically a loud volume) is generally referred to as being a 'power flam' and is a technique used extensively by drummers in all musical genres.

With reference to the feel of the groove in this section and throughout the track, focus on the balance and consistency of sounds between the hi-hat, ride cymbal (played in the C Section), snare drum and bass drum. Listen to how the groove locks in with the backing track. To become more familiar with the concept of the audio mix and balance of sounds, listen to the backing track of this arrangement (with drums) and also to the original recording, together with other songs in a similar style.

C Section (Measures 13–20)

In this section, the ride line continues with eighth notes and moves from the hi-hat to the ride cymbal. Notice the constant 'four on the floor' bass drum throughout the whole section, together with the sparse snare drum in measures 13–16, which becomes a 'two and four' backbeat, in unison with the bass drum, at measures 17–20.

D Section (Measures 21–28)

Be aware of anticipating the movement of the eighth notes from the ride cymbal in the previous section to the crash at measure 21, then to the hi-hat for the remainder of the section.

E Section (Measures 29–30)

The arrangement ends with a continuation of the groove and features a linear fill played through eighth notes between toms and bass drum, over beats 3 and 4 of measure 29 and through beats 1 and 2 of measure 30, finishing with a power flam on beat 3.

SONG TITLE: MAGGIE MAY
ALBUM: REASON TO BELIEVE
LABEL: MERCURY
GENRE: ROCK BALLAD

WRITTEN BY: ROD STEWART AND MARTIN QUITTENTON
PRODUCED BY: ROD STEWART

US CHART PEAK: 1

=125 *70's Rock*

A

BACKGROUND INFO

'Maggie May' was Rod Stewart's first hit single as a solo artist. The song was written by Rod Stewart in collaboration with guitarist Martin Quittenton and was featured on the 1971 album *Every Picture Tells a Story*. 'Maggie May' is about the ambivalent and contradictory emotions felt by a young man involved in a relationship with an older woman and is allegedly based on Stewart's experience.

'Maggie May' was the B side to 'Reason To Believe' but it attracted more interest and gained more airplay than the intended single. The song charted at no.1 on both sides of the Atlantic and launched Rod Stewart's solo career.

'Maggie May' was recorded in two takes in one session, but the cymbals were missing from the studio and so overdubbed at a later time. The album version features a thirty second guitar solo.

The drummer on 'Maggie May' was Micky Waller, a seasoned player known for his work with some of the biggest names on the UK's rock and blues scenes. He played with Little Richard on two UK tours, and also with Georgie Fame and The Steampacket, an outfit that featured Rod Stewart on vocals. He later joined John Mayall's Bluesbreakers for a short stint in a line up that included Peter Green and John McVie. Waller joined the Jeff Beck Group together with Rod Stewart, and the bassist in the group was Ron Wood (who would later join The Rolling Stones). This line up recorded the seminal album *Truth* – a huge success which set the way for Jeff Beck's solo career. Waller formed Silver Metre in 1969 and in the early 1970s he recorded with Stewart on his solo project. During the 1970s he worked with the Deluxe Blues Band and would go on to play with artists including The Walker Brothers, Cat Stevens, Eric Clapton, Bo Diddley, Dusty Springfield and Paul McCartney. He later formed the Micky Waller Band and played around the London area. During this period he also trained as a lawyer and used his expertise to fight court cases over unpaid royalties. Waller died aged 66 in 2008.

Other successful drummers who have worked with Stewart include Carmine Appice, Kenney Jones and David Palmer.

Maggie May

Rod Stewart

Words & Music by Rod Stewart & Martin Quittenton

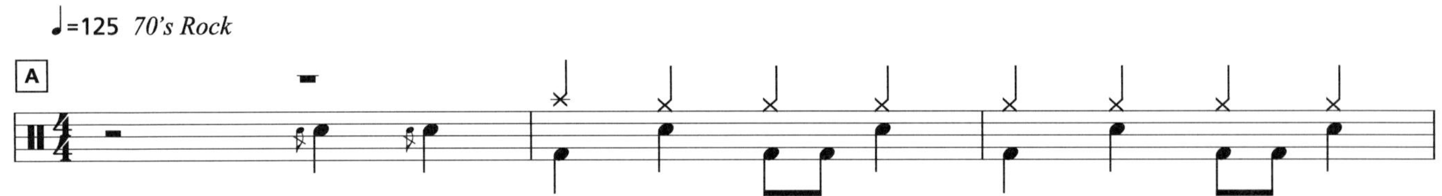

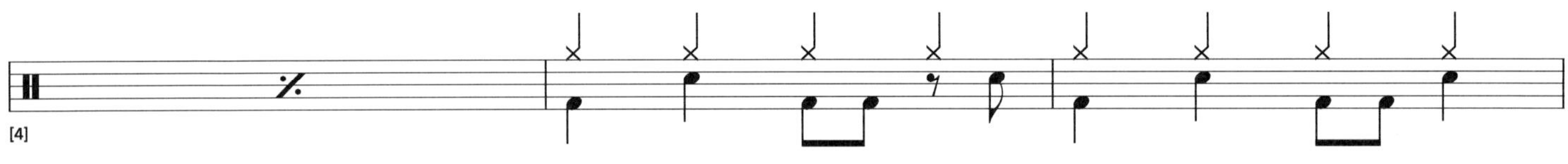

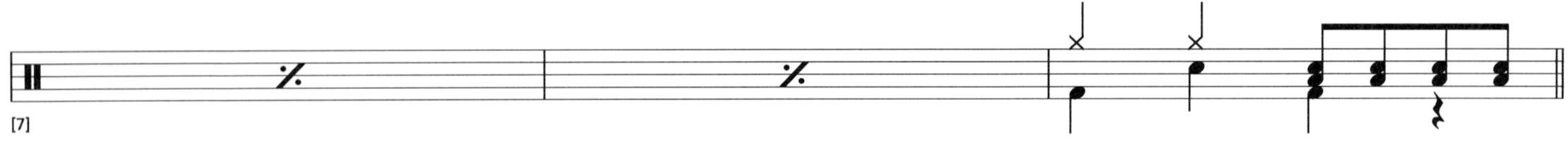

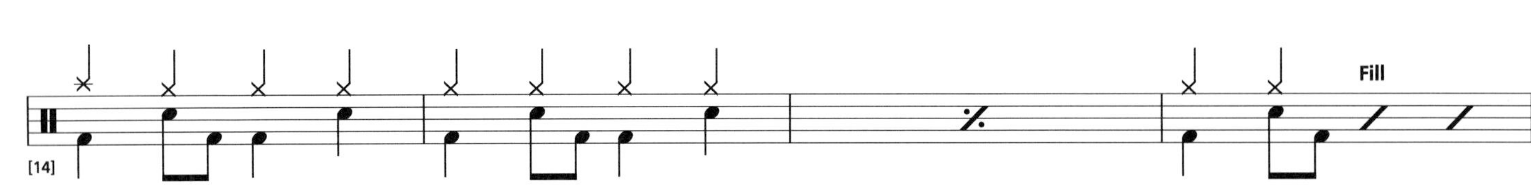

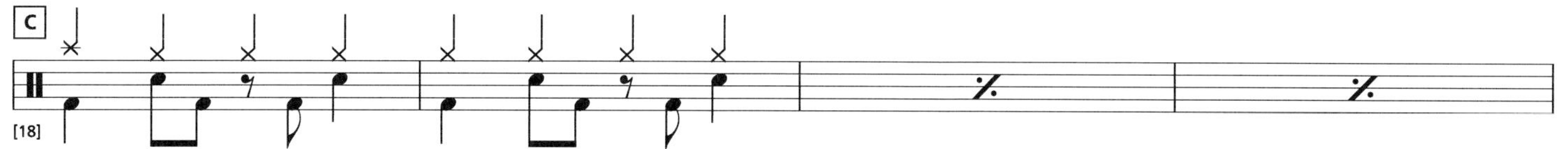
C
[18]

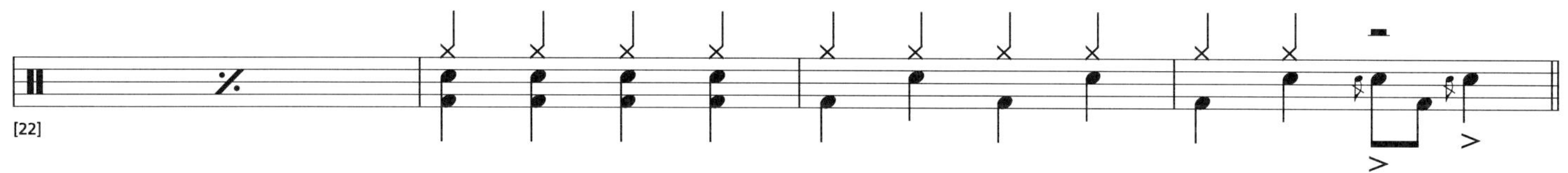
[22]

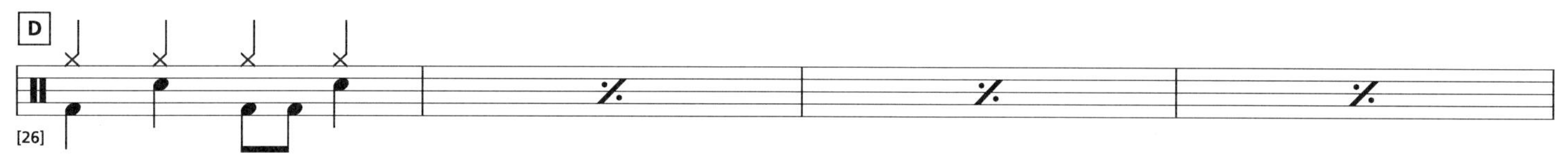
D
[26]

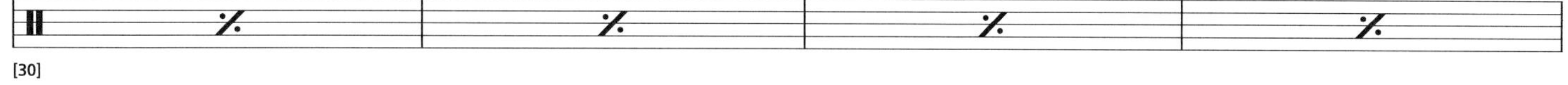
[30]

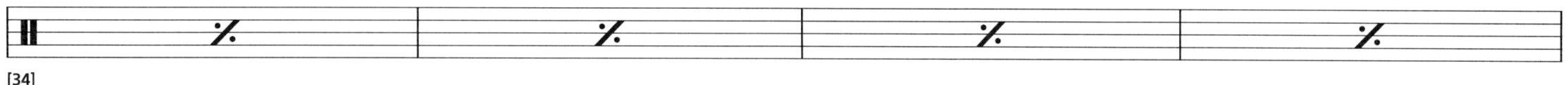
[34]

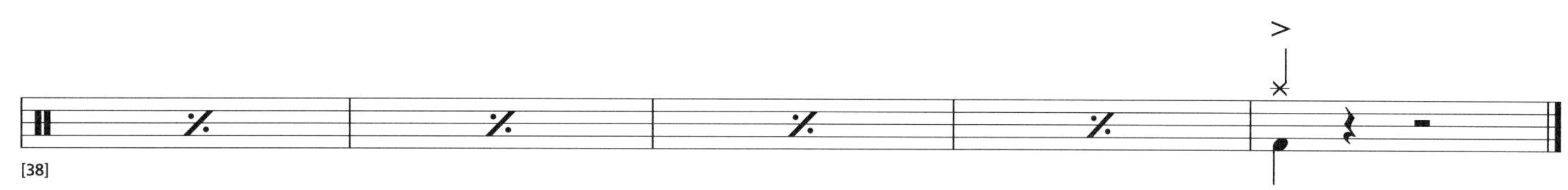
[38]

Walkthrough

Measure 1 | *Flam*
Snare drum flams are played on beats 3 and 4 of measure 1. A flam is a rudiment where one stick strikes fractionally before the other. Flams are one of the classic rudiments – they are very good for wrist development and can be employed in many styles of music. Experiment with different sticking for these notes. It could be an alternating flam which means to reverse the sticking i.e. lR going to rL. Alternatively, don't reverse the second flam, i.e. lR lR. Choose the sticking which sounds the best and feels most confident to you. Flams are used again in measure 26.

Measure 2 | *Crash cymbal on beat 1*
A very effective drumming device (often used to indicate a change of section or beginning/end of a piece) is to play the crash cymbal on the first beat. Play the crash confidently and make sure that the bass drum sounds at exactly the same time and not before or after the crash cymbal.

Measures 2–16 | *Snare and bass drum variations*
Measure 2 contains the first groove pattern which appears throughout the piece. The hi-hat plays a quarter note pulse which drives the rhythm forward whilst the snare drum plays a solid backbeat rhythm. The bass drum is playing on beat 1 and then two consecutive eighth notes on beat 3. If this is difficult, remember that the first bass drum sounds in unison with the hi-hat. The second falls in the gap before the next hi-hat and snare drum unison note.

Measure 5 | *Snare drum displacement*
In measure 5 there is snare drum displacement. Instead of the snare playing on beat 4 it is placed on the following eighth note. Between measures 14 and 17 the bass drum rhythm changes. Here the bass drum is played on beat 1 & 3, and the off-beat of beat 2. Another way to describe this is that the bass drum is played in the gap after the snare drum has been played for the first time. This can be a co-ordination challenge as the bass drum is playing two consecutive
notes with the second one falling underneath the hi-hat quarter-note.

Measure 17 | *Time slashes and fill*
Measure 17 sees the first use of time slashes with the word "fill" written above. This means play a stylistically appropriate fill over two quarter note beats. Here is an opportunity to improvise a fill which communicates the direction and feel of the music.

Measures 18–22 | *Extra snare and bass drum variations*
In measure 18 the bass drum pattern changes. Here we are playing on beat 1 and the off-beats of 2 and 3. To play this accurately, you could count all the eighth notes "One and two and three and four and". Play the bass drum on the "one" and then the "and" of beats 2 and 3. If this proves tricky, slow the tempo down and work on each quarter note beat in isolation before putting each part back together. It is worth noting that in measure 22 the crash cymbal is used again to announce a change of groove.

Measure 23 | *Unison phrase*
In measure 23 all three voices are written in unison on each quarter note. Make sure all notes are played exactly together and not fractionally apart. Try to make all three voices be as one sound.

Measure 27 | *One measure repeat*
From measure 27 there is a one-measure repeat to indicate playing the same groove pattern repeatedly. This diagonal line with dots side by side is commonly seen on many drum charts.

Measure 42 | *Crash cymbal conclusion*
The final measure is enhanced by the use of the crash cymbal and bass drum together on beat 1. This firmly indicates the conclusion of the arrangement.

SONG TITLE: GEORGIA ON MY MIND
ALBUM: THE GENIUS HITS THE ROAD
LABEL: ABC PARAMOUNT
GENRE: RHYTHM AND BLUES
WRITTEN BY: HOAGY CARMICHAEL AND STUART GORRELL
PRODUCED BY: SID FELLER
US CHART PEAK: 1

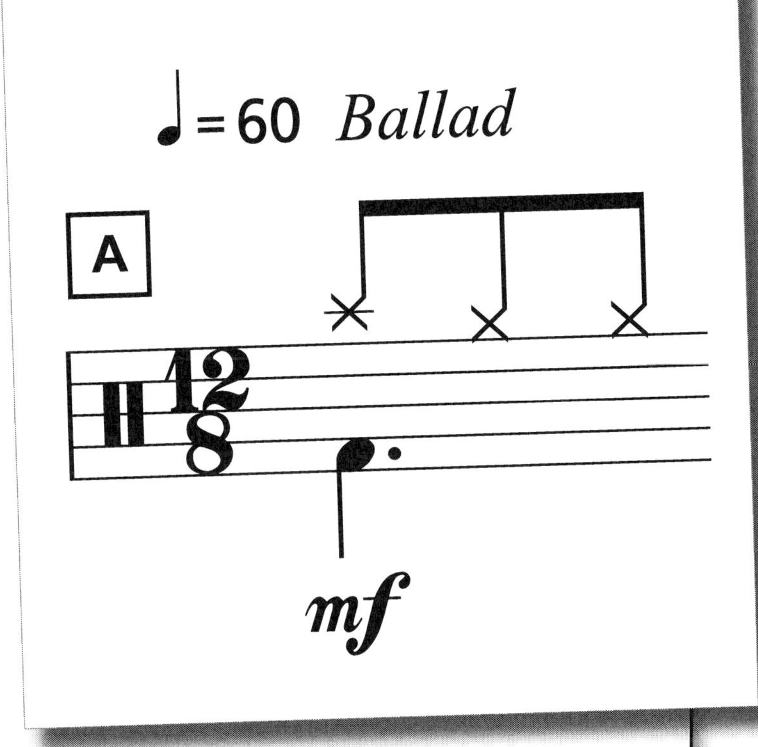

BACKGROUND INFO

'Georgia On My Mind', released in 1960, was Ray Charles' first single for ABC-Paramount. The song was featured on the album *The Genius Hits The Road* which received national acclaim and won four Grammy Awards including Best Vocal Performance Single Record or Track, Male and Best Performance by a Pop Single Artist for 'Georgia On My Mind'. It was Charles' first collaboration with Sid Feller who produced, arranged and conducted the recording. Charles followed the success of 'Georgia On My Mind' with 'Hit The Road Jack' and the increase in royalties and show fees this produced allowed him to expand his group from a small road ensemble to a touring big band. In addition, he gained greater creative control of his output. These were highly unusual circumstances for a black artist at the time.

'Georgia On My Mind' was originally released as a single in 1930 by Hoagy Carmichael but it has become associated with Ray Charles after the huge success his version achieved. It was also released by Willie Nelson in 1978, winning a Grammy Award. The song has been adopted by the state of Georgia as its official song.

'Georgia On My Mind' is amongst Ray Charles' most revered recordings. The list also includes 'I Got a Woman', 'What'd I Say', 'Hit The Road Jack' and 'Unchain My Heart'. All of these songs have, in turn, been covered by many different artists both live and in the studio. Joe Cocker had a very successful single with his version of 'Unchain My Heart' in 1987 and John Mayer covered 'I Got A Woman' achieving great success.

Through his foundations, and personal contributions, Ray Charles donated significant amounts of money to institutions associated with the research of hearing disorders. He explained that giving to this cause, rather than to the research of visual impairment, was due to music saving his life and being certain he wouldn't know what to do if he could not experience it.

Ray Charles was a significant figure during the Civil Rights Movement era. He received a Grammy Lifetime Achievement Award in 1991 and was one of the first inductees to the Rock and Roll Hall of Fame at its inaugural ceremony in 1986. Ray Charles died, aged 73, in 2003. His influence remains undiminished.

Georgia On My Mind

Ray Charles
Words by Stuart Gorrell

B

[17]

[19]

[21]

[23]

[25]

[27]

[29]

[31]

[33]

[35]

Walkthrough

Rhythm Pattern

This arrangement of 'Georgia On My Mind' uses a slow tempo triplet ballad feel in 6/8 time. The eighth note time feel is played on both the hi-hat in the A section and the ride cymbal from letter B. When practicing, make sure that the triplet sub-division is evenly played and that there is space between the notes. Count each of the eighth-note triplets out loud: "One triplet, two triplet, three triplet, four triplet".

Once this is under control, play the different parts of the kit whilst counting out loud simultaneously. This counting method can be very effective in developing good time-keeping skills. First, try the cymbal rhythm with the count, then the bass drum, and then the snare drum. When each part is feeling comfortable in isolation, put them together until all parts can be played whilst counting out-loud at the same time.

To further improve the rhythm, dynamic shaping can be added. The four dotted quarter notes found within the beat should have a strong feeling and each be relatively equal in sound. The notes found in the gaps can be played a little lighter. Pay attention to the internal dynamics of the groove and how each drum kit part relates to the other. Avoid any flamming between instruments and make sure individual notes are consistent from measure to measure.

It is a good idea to record yourself practising this rhythm so that the sound can be analysed during playback.

Song Form and Fill Technique

'Georgia On My Mind' is a 32 measure song form. There are two sections both of which are 16 measures long. On the chart these are labelled at the start of each 16 measures as A and B. A song form which consists of two sixteen measure sections is sometimes described as being "two sixteens" when discussing structure with other musicians.

After the main melody has been played there is an outro which is three measures in length and contains a simple fill, orchestrated on the snare drum and the high and floor tom. Single sticking is suggested to navigate the fill, and don't forget to close the hi-hat so it doesn't ring on.

'Georgia On My Mind' may prove particularly challenging if you are less familiar with compound time grooves. It is also likely that this arrangement is slower than most of the music you have encountered so far, so remember to feel the sub-division and be patient as over time slower tempos will become more comfortable. Tempo and technique can be improved by listening and playing to a variety of recordings which feature this classic groove, so search through your music collection for similar songs and add slow tempos to your practice routine.

Bugzy Malone

SONG TITLE: RELEGATION RIDDIM
ALBUM: RELEASED AS SINGLE
LABEL: SONUS MUSIC / ZDOT PRODUCTIONS LTD.
GENRE: GRIME

WRITTEN BY: AARON DAVIS
PRODUCED BY: BUGZY MALONE

US CHART PEAK: N/A

BACKGROUND INFO

Bugzy Malone, real name Aaron Davis, has quickly established himself as a rising star in the grime genre, breaking the trend of London or Midlands-based artists dominating the scene. Bugzy Malone's deeply introspective lyrics have been highlighted by many critics and listeners and are a significant factor in his craft, setting him apart from other grime artists.

This is no surprise seeing that Davis arrived at music scarred from a past riddled with the complications of a dysfunctional upbringing and his family being torn apart, as he put it, by career criminals. He dropped out of school and by the time of his GSCEs he was in prison. Due to his physical prowess and athleticism, boxing looked like a possible avenue to straighten himself out. However, his creativity was ready to resurface.

Music entered Davis' life as a redeeming vehicle for creativity and self-expression. In addition to the poignancy of his lyrical vocal style, his Mancunian accent makes his work immediately recognisable and fresh. His style blends a confessional narrative delivered clearly and confidently with occasional bursts of fast and technical rap. He began rapping to the *Risky Roadz* DVD series, as did Dizzee Rascal, Wiley and Skepta, whom Davis counts amongst his influences.

Bugzy Malone has released three EPs to date and five mix tapes between 2010 and 2015. His first commercial album release was *King Of The North* peaking at no.4 in the UK charts. This was followed by *B. Inspired*, released in 2018. Bugzy Malone is currently promoting his work with live shows in the UK and Europe mainly backed by computer tracks.

Relegation Riddim

Bugzy Malone
Words & Music by Aaron Davies & Thomas Broderick

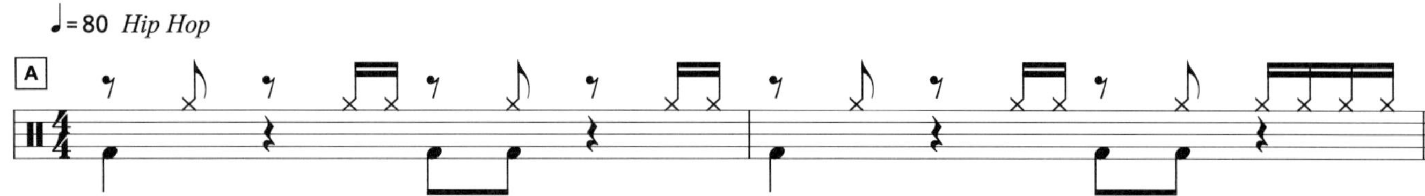

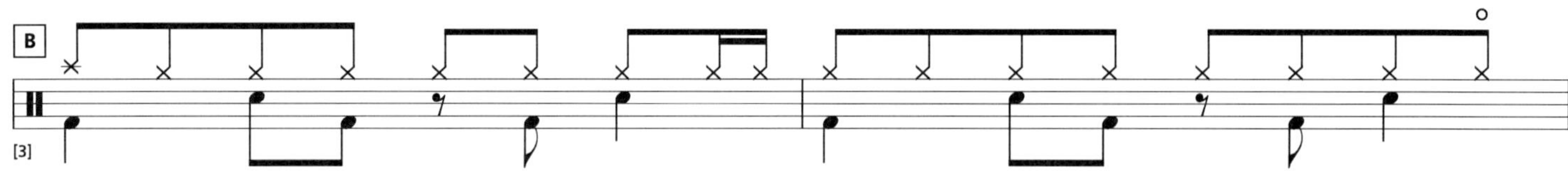

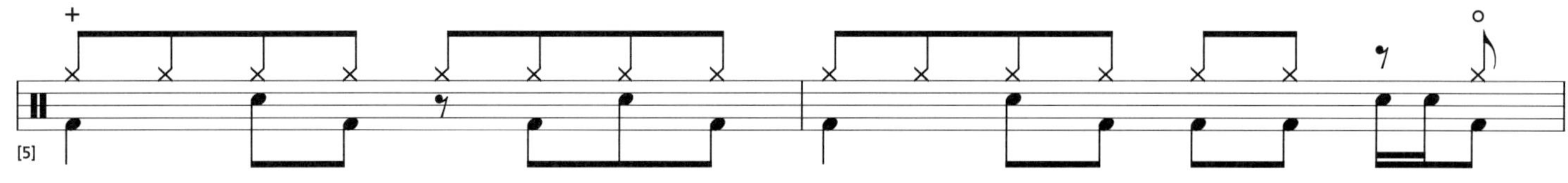

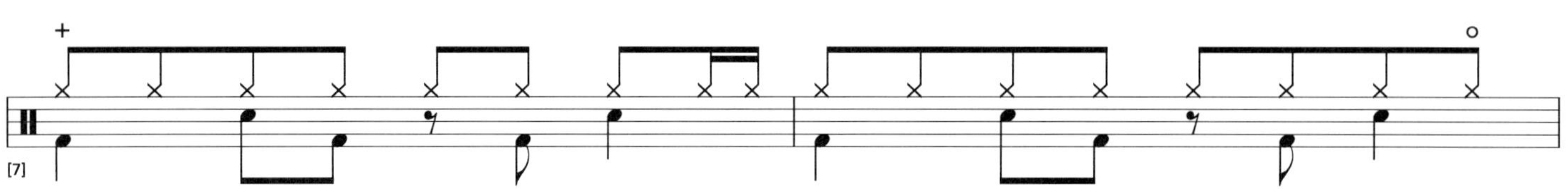

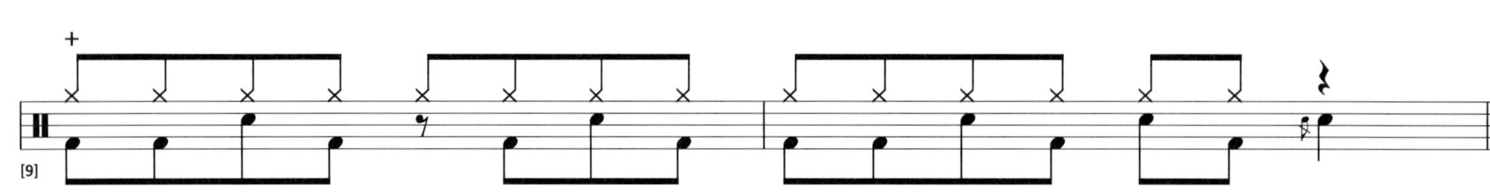

C

[11]

[13]

[15]

[17]

D

[19]

[21]

Walkthrough

A Section (Measures 1–2)

This hip hop track begins with a two-measure introduction and features some spacious interplay between hi-hat and bass drum. While not necessarily technically difficult to play, this opening section does present certain challenges with regard to co-ordination and time-keeping.

To lock in with the time-feel of the track, it's always advisable to count and prepare the time flow internally before the drums come in. Given the slow tempo, it's best to feel and count 16th notes (counted as "1 e & a, 2 e & a.." etc.), which of course also includes eighth notes (1 & 2 & 3 & 4 &). This will help to internalise and develop the timing, flow and consistency of the groove.

With regard to co-ordination, pay attention to where the hi-hat and bass drum figures fall and to the space between the figures. Feeling and counting the rests is just as important as playing the figures.

The 16th notes on the hi-hat, over beat 4 of measure 2, should be played with a hand-to-hand sticking, to prepare for the crash cymbal at the beginning of the B Section.

B Section (Measures 3–10)

This section features a predominant eighth note groove on the hi-hat, together with snare backbeats and bass drum variations. Notice the 16th-note embellishments of the ride line at the end of measures 3 and 7. Again, these 16th notes can be played hand-to-hand for technical ease - or can be played single handed, if that feels technically and physically comfortable.

In general, pay attention to the co-ordination of the bass drum variations and snare drum backbeats – all of which fall in unison with the hi-hat eighth notes. Those unisons should fall together, so be careful not to flam.

Notice the open and closed hi-hat figures in measures 4–9, including the 16th-note fill at the end of measure 6. Be positive and make a good connection with the stick when opening and closing the hi-hat cymbals. Also, be sure to keep the foot in contact with the pedal board, to maintain control.

This section ends with a single 'power flam' on beat 4 of measure 10. It's important that the flam is played as a flam, not as a unison. Be positive and play each note of the flam powerfully, at the same volume.

With reference to the feel of the groove in this section and throughout the track, focus on the dynamic balance and consistency of sounds between the hi-hat, ride cymbal (played in the C Section), snare drum and bass drum. Listen to how the groove locks in with the click and backing track.

C Section (Measures 11–18)

Measures 11–14 feature a ride cymbal breakdown of eighth note and 16th-note figures. Again, the 16th notes in ride cymbal figures can be played single or double-handed – whichever feels most comfortable. Measure 12 ends with a power flam and measure 14 ends with 16th note snare fill over beat 4, leading in to the crash cymbal at measure 17.

Measures 15–17 settles in to a predominant eighth-note groove and features a tom fill, around 16th note figures, over beats 2 and 3 of measure 18, finishing with a backbeat on beat 4.

D Section (Measures 19–22)

Be aware of the crash cymbal when coming in to measure 19, then stay on the hi-hat for the remainder of the groove. Notice the 16th-note hi-hat embellishments in measure 19, together with open and closed figures in measures 20–21 respectively.

The arrangement ends on measure 22 with a fill played between unison toms and bass drum, through an eighth note and 16th-note rhythmic phrase and finishing on the snare.

SONG TITLE: BLEACH
GENRE: MODERN ROCK
TEMPO: 110 BPM

TECH FEATURES: FLAMS
HI-HAT FOOT
OPEN HI-HAT GROOVE

COMPOSERS: JAMES UINGS &
KUNG FU DRUMMER

PERSONNEL: JAMES UINGS (GTR/BASS)
NOAM LEDERMAN (DRUMS)

OVERVIEW

'Bleach' is a track inspired by emo bands such as My Chemical Romance, Jimmy Eat World and Fall Out Boy. It features hard rock beats accentuated with heavy flam driven accents played around the kit in unison with dynamic guitar stabs.

STYLE FOCUS

The emo rock drumming style relies upon the drummer exuding great musicianship and having a repertoire of different rhythms to complement the various emotions conveyed by the vocals and guitars. You will need to lock in tight with the music because there is little room for error when emphasising stabs at slow to medium tempos. The drums and bass will lock down the tempo of the song while the guitars play melodies over the top. Some verse sections may only contain drums, bass and vocals, with the guitars held back for the choruses. Confidence and precision when playing are essential to this style.

THE BIGGER PICTURE

Emo began in the 1980s when groups like Rites Of Spring and Embrace were labelled emotional hardcore (hardcore is an offshoot of punk and rock). Their music was more expressive than that of other hardcore bands and was accompanied by melodic guitars and varied rhythms.

In 1993, American band Jimmy Eat World formed and in 2001 brought emo to the masses with their fourth album *Bleed American*, which became a multi-platinum seller. The four-piece were one of the cornerstones of emo rock and have inspired a slew of other bands, some of which have added an even harder rock edge to the sound such as Brand New.

The 2000s belonged to My Chemical Romance whose own brand of emo incorporated a dramatic stage presence and dark lyrical content.

RECOMMENDED LISTENING

Start with *Bleed American*; in particular, the title track and 'The Middle', both of which feature solid drumming from Zach Lind. My Chemical Romance's *The Black Parade* (2006) is also worth listening to. Hits like 'Welcome To The Black Parade' and 'Famous Last Words' demonstrate their musical versatility. More recently, *Danger Days: The True Lives Of The Fabulous Killjoys* (2010) displays the group's change of direction and a range of drummers.

Bleach

James Uings & Kung Fu Drummer

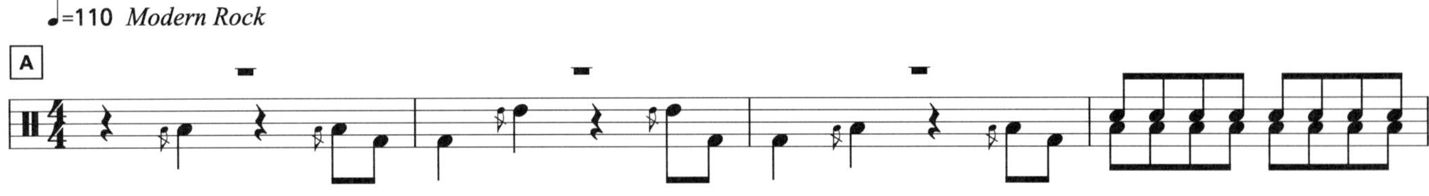

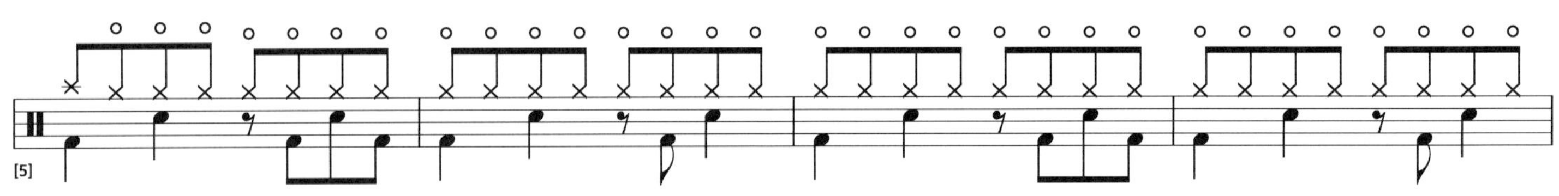

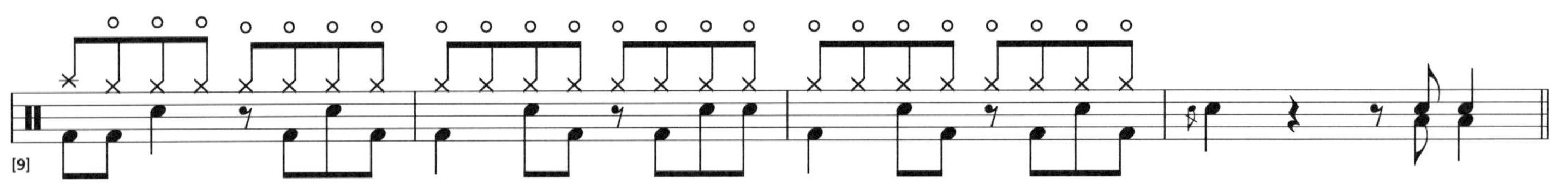

B

[13]

[17]

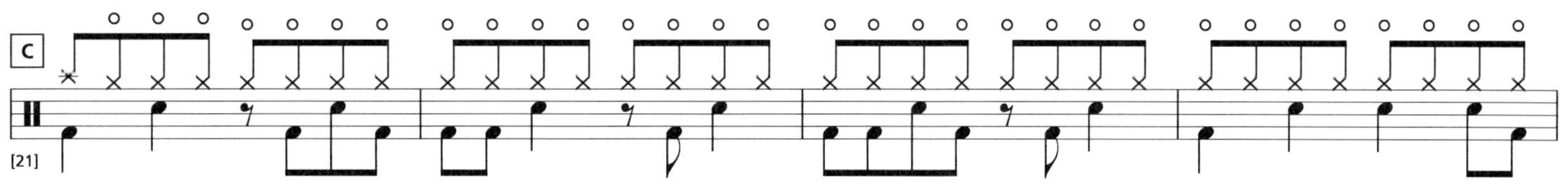
C
[21]

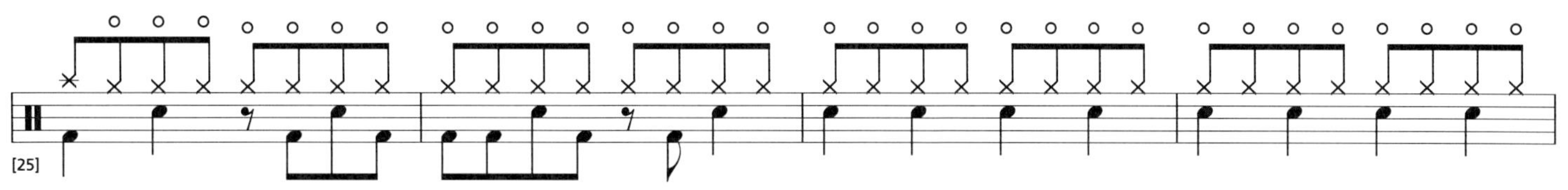
[25]

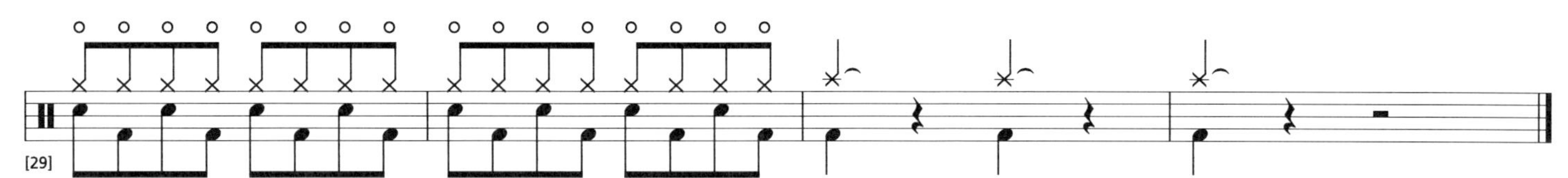
[29]

Walkthrough

A Section (Measures 1–12)

The first three measures feature flams on the backbeat with occasional bass drums. In the fourth measure, a fill signals the arrival of the full groove in measure 5. The groove consists of eighth note open hi-hats and bass/snare drum variations.

Measures 1–3 | *Backbeat flams*
Play the flams in these measures on the backbeat (the second and fourth beats). When performing flams on the kit, ensure that your hands are well placed to achieve the grace note/full stroke combination.

Measure 4 | *Unison fill*
In this measure, there are consistent eighth notes played on the floor tom and snare drum. You can achieve consistency of sound and 'togetherness' by lifting both hands to the same height before hitting the surface of the drum. The concept of togetherness is also known as unison (Fig. 1).

Measure 5 | *Open hi-hat groove*
The hi-hat in this groove is played in the open position. Loosen your foot that holds the hi-hat pedal to create the open hi-hat sound and aim for consistency. Remember that your hi-hat foot needs to remain in contact with the pedal at all times. Taking it off will affect your posture and timing.

Measures 5–11 | *Snare and bass variations*
In this section, there are many variations of the bass and snare drum pattern. Try practising this pattern (the lower part of the stave) without the cymbals initially and make sure that all of the rhythmic values are accurate.

Measure 12 | *Break and fill*
On the first beat of this measure there is a quarter-note flam on the snare, then a beat and a half rest followed by a fill on the offbeat of the third beat and the fourth beat. Counting the rests between the break and fill maintains continuity and develops a stronger sense of pulse. The two stroke fill on snare and floor tom should follow the unison principle.

B Section (Measures 13–20)

The first six measures of this section are similar to the opening of the piece but with the addition of the hi-hat foot on each beat. Measures 19 and 20 consist of a long preparation fill for the arrival of the groove in measure 21.

Measures 13–18 | *Co-ordinating with the left foot*
Your hands primarily play backbeat flams in these measures. Aim to get this pattern synchronised accurately with your hi-hat foot and then work on the variations in measures 14 and 16.

Measures 13–18 | *Hi-hat foot*
Your hi-hat foot should be played on every beat in these measures. Aim to perform the movement with accuracy and conviction to avoid any unnecessary splashing sounds. There are two techniques that can be used when attempting a hi-hat foot pattern: heel up and heel down. Use the technique that suits you best and feels more comfortable to execute. With both techniques, your foot should always remain in contact with the hi-hat pedal.

C Section (Measures 21–32)

The groove in this section is similar to the one that began in measure 5, but develops from measure 27 and leads to the final crash hits in measures 31 and 32.

Measures 27–30 | *Snare on every beat*
In this groove, there is a quarter-note snare on every beat. The eighth note open hi-hats should remain even throughout the section. This type of groove creates more intensity in the drums and can therefore lead to speeding up. Keep the pulse steady and ensure a consistent sound is produced from each part of the kit played (Fig. 2).

Measures 31–32 | *Sound production: crash cymbal*
In order to produce the best sound from the crash cymbal, allow your hand to bounce back after hitting the cymbal and be careful that your grip of the stick is not too tight. Leaving the stick on the cymbal surface for too long can choke the cymbal and affect its natural decay. In order to achieve a convincing sound from the crash, try playing with the neck part of your drum stick.

Fig. 1: Unison fill

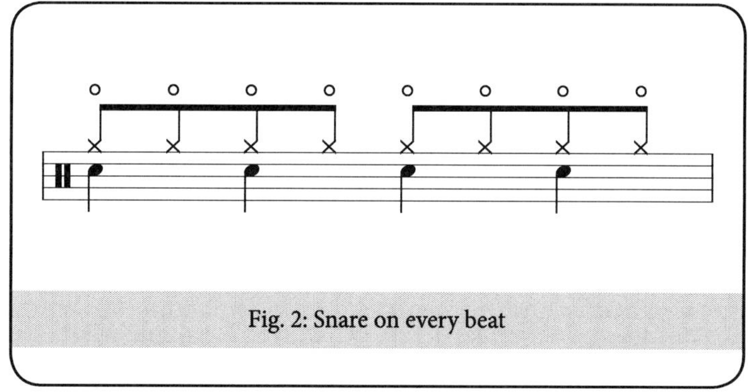
Fig. 2: Snare on every beat

Dora And Bootsy

SONG TITLE: DORA AND BOOTSY
GENRE: FUNK
TEMPO: 105 BPM

TECH FEATURES: EIGHTH-NOTE TRIPLETS
SNARE & TOM FILLS
UNISON BASS AND SNARE

COMPOSER: LUKE ALDRIDGE

PERSONNEL: STUART RYAN (GTR)
HENRY THOMAS (BASS)
NOAM LEDERMAN (DRUMS)
ROSS STANLEY (KEYS)
FULL FAT HORNS (BRASS)
FERGUS GERRAND (PERC)

OVERVIEW

'Dora And Bootsy' is a funk track written in the style of the legendary and flamboyant bass player Bootsy Collins. Collins began his career in the 1970s playing with funk and soul artists including James Brown, George Clinton's Parliament-Funkadelic and with his own group Bootsy's Rubber Band. This funk flavoured track incorporates drum techniques and features like flams, open hi-hat, and unison bass and snare among others.

STYLE FOCUS

The focus of funk is rhythm. With this in mind, don't be fooled by the simplicity of some funk grooves because even the simplest of ideas must be played to a high standard to create a fluid funk sound. A groove has to be solid to capture the essence of funk; you will hear that demonstrated on this track where the bass drum and the bassline lock in on the A section.

THE BIGGER PICTURE

Funk developed from soul, R&B and blues during the 1960s. These earlier styles used a backbeat (the snare on beats 2 and 4) but funk uses a greater degree of syncopation and an emphasis on the first beat or, as it is known in funk circles, 'the one'. Brown is said to have created funk with the release of his single 'Cold Sweat' in 1967, which featured this emphasis. In the early 1970s, Brown worked with a band named The J.B.s, an outfit that included Bootsy Collins and drummer John 'Jabo' Starks among many other musicians, some of whom went on to join George Clinton's Parliament-Funkadelic. Their influence can be heard in the music of more contemporary groups like the jazz and funk jam band Galactic (featuring drummer Stanton Moore) who mix classic funk styles with modern elements.

RECOMMENDED LISTENING

Brown's drummers Clyde Stubblefield, Melvin Parker and John 'Jabo' Starks are essential listening for those looking to progress in funk. Classic tracks 'Cold Sweat', 'Funky Drummer' and 'Sex Machine' are standouts, but then the majority of Brown's catalogue throws up many gems. The Parliament-Funkadelic songs 'One Nation Under A Groove' and 'Up For The Down Stroke' capture the band in full funk flow. To hear the P-Funk influence in a more contemporary context, listen to Galactic's 2007 album *From The Corner To The Block* and *Rage!* (2008) by Lettuce, showcasing the talents of drummer Adam Deitch.

Dora And Bootsy

Luke Aldridge

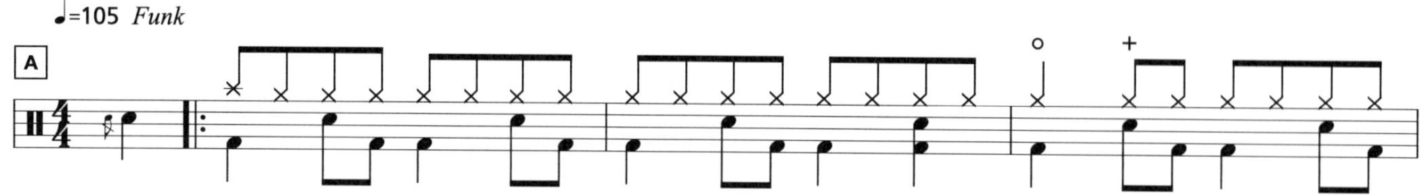

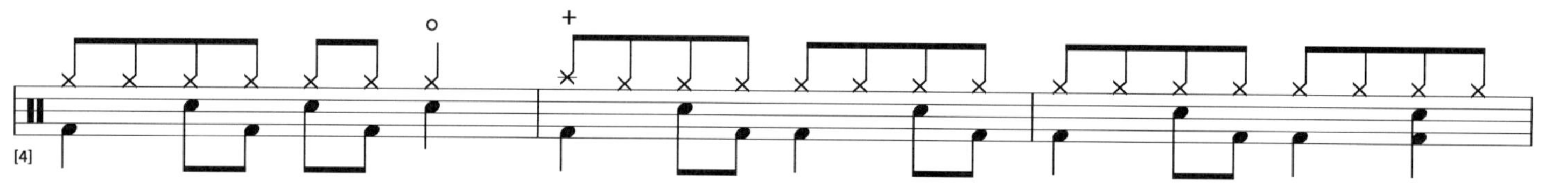

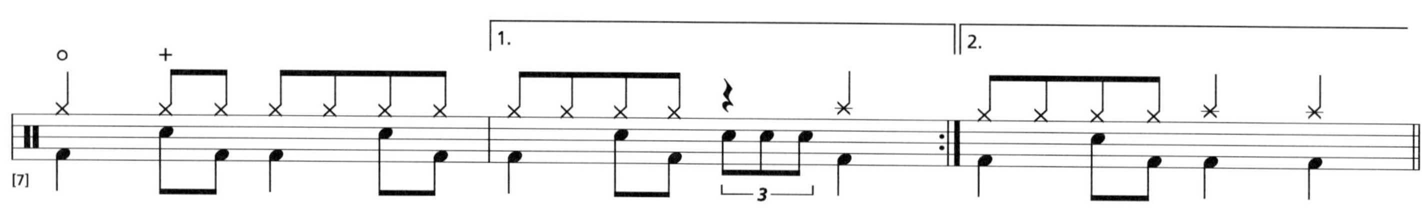

B

[10]

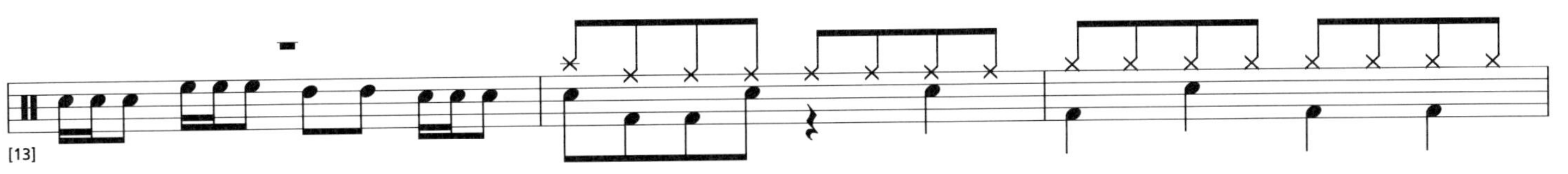
[13]

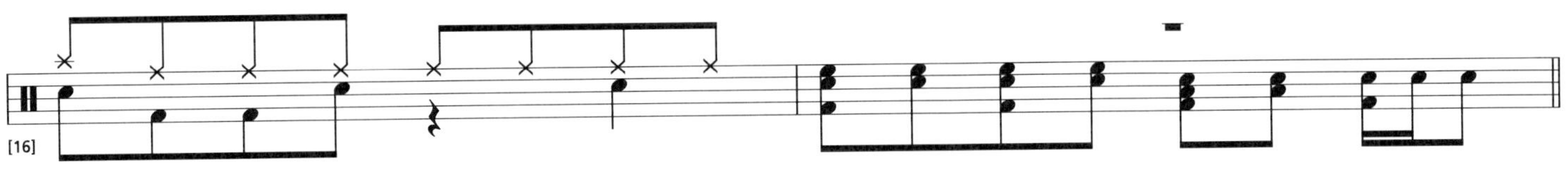
[16]

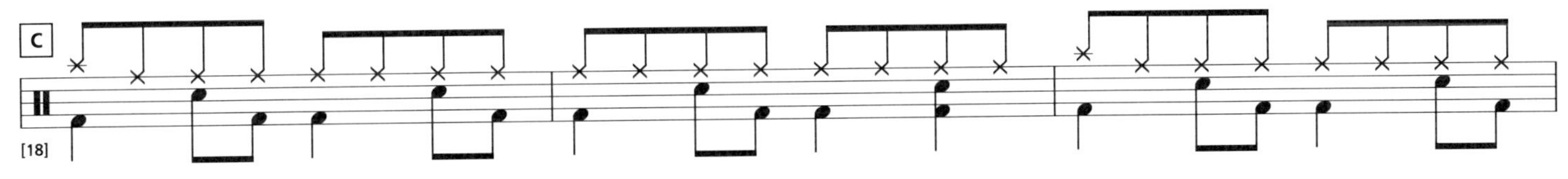
C
[18]

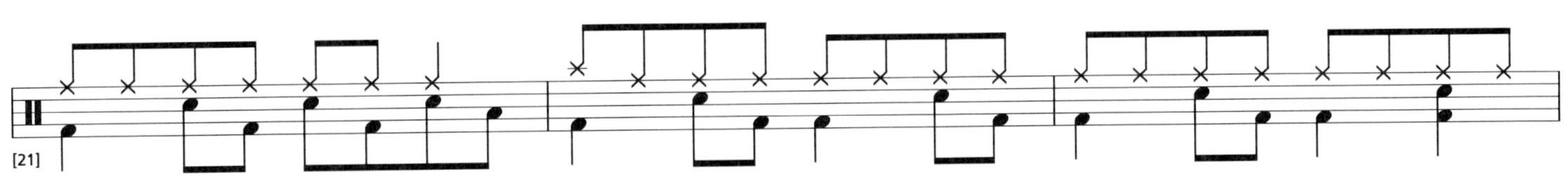
[21]

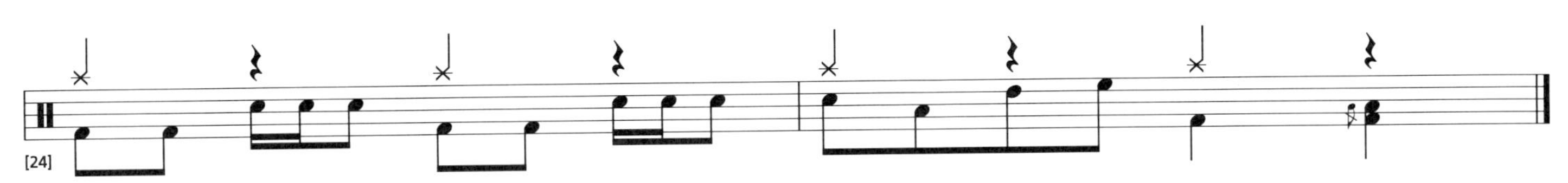
[24]

Walkthrough

A Section (Measures 1–9)

The first section of this piece features a funky groove with open hi-hats. In measure 8, there is a repeat sign indicating that measures 1–7 should be played again. After playing this section for the second time, skip the first time measure and continue directly to this second time measure.

Pick-up measure | *Counting the pick-up*
In this piece, there is a pick-up snare flam before the groove starts in measure 1. The snare flam is placed on the last beat of the spoken count in (i.e. the fourth beat of the second measure).

Measure 3 | *Quarter-note open hi-hat*
The open hi-hat in this measure is opened on beat 1 and should only close on beat 2. This means that the open hi-hat sound needs to ring for a full value of a quarter note. Practise the hi-hat pattern until you achieve fluency then co-ordinate it with the snare and bass drum.

Measure 5 | *Closing the hi-hat*
The '+' above the crash cymbal note indicates that the hi-hat should be closed while playing the crash at the same time.

Measure 8 | *Triplet fill*
The fill in the second part of measure 8 includes an eighth-note triplet on the snare. In a triplet, all three notes should be even. As these are eighth-note triplets, they are played in the space of one quarter note. There are many sticking options that will lead you to the crash on the fourth beat. However, the first stage is deciding whether you prefer hitting the crash with your right or left hand. Both sticking options are shown above the triplet on the third beat of Fig. 1.

B Section (Measures 10–17)

The groove changes in this section, offering many variations and fills that allow the drummer to shine.

Measure 10 | *Groove*
This groove is a musical interpretation of the parts played by the other instruments. The unorthodox snare and bass drum pattern may be hard to co-ordinate at first, but if played convincingly this is an impressive funky drum moment.

Measure 11 | *Groove variation*
In this measure, the snare plays on the third beat and the bass drum on the other three. Try playing measures 10 and 11 repeatedly and aim for fluent movement between the ride or crash cymbal and the hi-hat.

Measure 13 | *Fill*
This fill is based on the rhythmic phrase of two 16th notes and an eighth note. This phrase is used on every beat apart from the third where only two eighth notes are to be played. Because 16th notes are most commonly counted as "1 e & a 2 e & a", count the phrase used here as "1 e & 2 e &". Although you are not playing on the "a", the value of this 16th note should be preserved. Once you understand the rhythms in this measure, look at the voices used and practise moving around the toms with confidence and a solid pulse (Fig. 2).

Measure 17 | *Unison fill*
Your ability to play this fill well will depend on your achieving accurate unison between the drums. Start with the hands pattern and cut out unnecessary flams between the snare and toms then add the bass drum and focus on the balance (your natural tendency will be to play the bass drum louder than the snare and toms).

C Section (Measures 18–25)

This is a reprise of the A section but the groove is played on the ride cymbal.

Throughout | *Sound production*
In order to produce the best sound from the drums, it is important to keep in mind some fundamental principles. The snare and toms should be struck in the middle of the drum head. After hitting a drum, allow your hand to bounce back. Ensure that your grip on the stick is not too tight and allows the stick some movement.

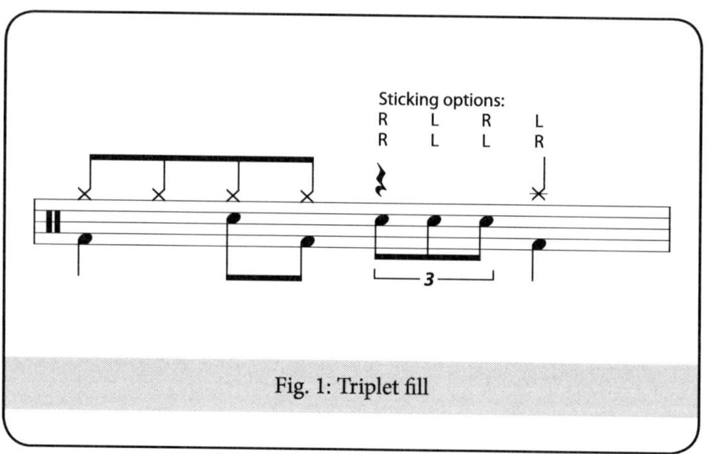

Fig. 1: Triplet fill

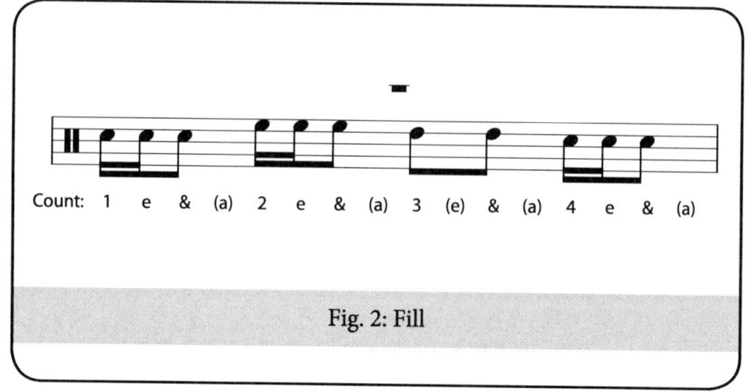

Fig. 2: Fill

SONG TITLE: CUBA MAMA
GENRE: MAMBO
TEMPO: 120 BPM

TECH FEATURES: HI-HAT FOOT CONTROL
FOUR-WAY COORDINATION
FLAMS ON TOMS

COMPOSER: NOAM LEDERMAN

PERSONNEL: NOAM LEDERMAN (DRUMS)
HENRY THOMAS (BASS)
FERGUS GERRAND (PERC)
KISHON KHAN (PIANO)
JAKE PAINTER (TRUMPET)

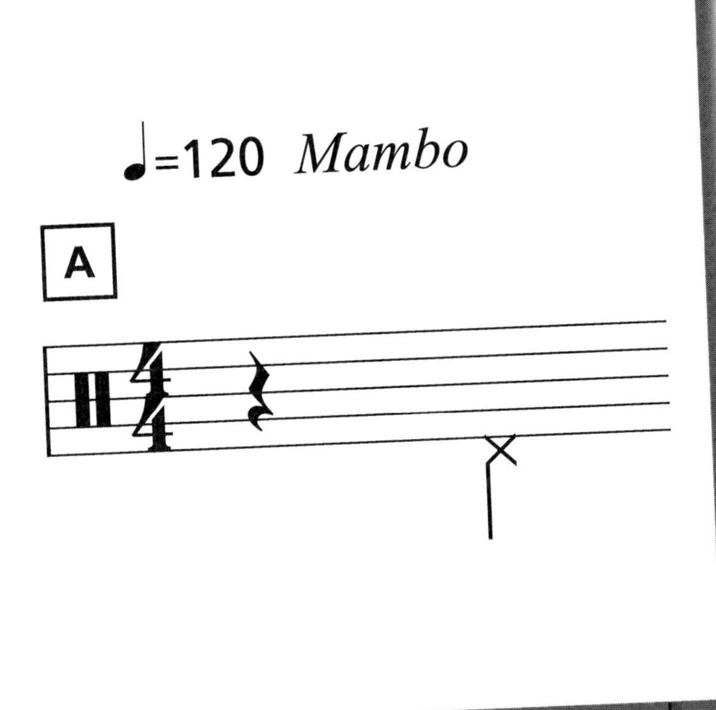

OVERVIEW

'Cuba Mama' is a mambo piece written in the style of Israel 'Cachao' López, the inventor of the mambo rhythm, and that of his fellow Cubans Pérez Prado and Buena Vista Social Club. It features hi-hat foot control, four-way coordination and tom flams.

STYLE FOCUS

Traditionally, the drum kit did not feature in mambo music. The drum beats that have been created since its birth are a mixture of the various percussion patterns of the style. Each drum voice represents a percussive sound and an essential rhythmic figure. Modern Latin drummers have developed these elements into beats requiring four-way coordination.

THE BIGGER PICTURE

Cuban bassist 'Cachao' Lopez invented the mambo rhythm with his brother Orestes in the 1930s. Mambo was considered too radical at first and it took the efforts of band leader Pérez Prado to give the genre a mainstream audience. Although mambo was played mostly in Cuba and Mexico, interest in the genre grew in New York in the 1950s. A mambo dance craze spread and bands such as Tito Rodriquez and Tito Puente performed at fast tempos that suited dancers.

By the 1990s, interest in mambo had dwindled. Hollywood actor Andy Garcia organised recording sessions with leading Cuban musicians in an attempt to preserve Cuba's musical heritage. The result was an album entitled *Cachao Master Session Volume I/ II*, which won a Grammy award. This project was the basis of the documentary film *Cachao: Como Su Ritmo No Hay Dos* (Cachao: Like His Rhythm There Is No Other), which resurrected Lopez's career.

In 1999, American musician and composer Ry Cooder produced the film and documentary *Buena Vista Social Club* to offer a glimpse into the Cuban music scene.

RECOMMENDED LISTENING

Mambo's creator 'Cachao' López is heard best on *Cuba Linda* (2000) and the Grammy award-winning *Ahora Si!* (2004). Pérez Prado has several 'best of' albums and *Prez* (1958) is one of his most accomplished recordings. Ry Cooder's production of *Buena Vista Social Club* (1997) shows another side to the music of Cuba and includes the vocal talent of Ibrahim Ferrer and Compay Segundo.

Cuba Mama

Noam Lederman

♩=120 *Mambo*

A

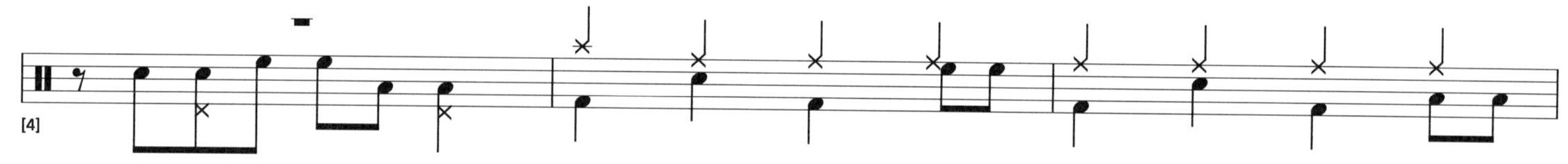

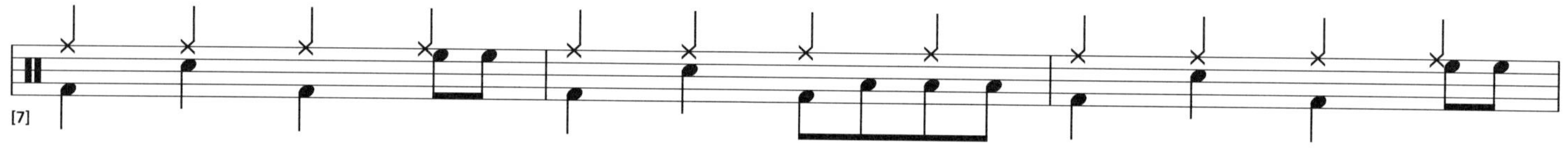

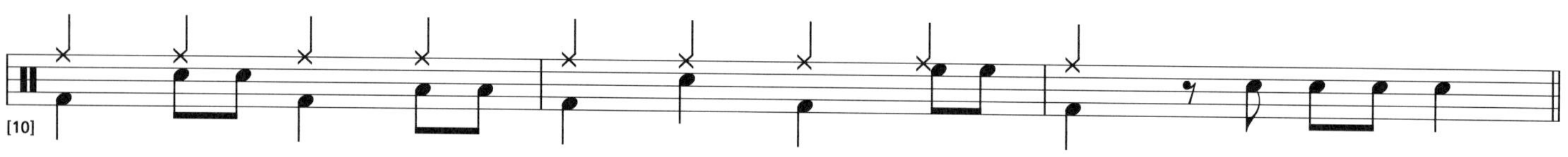

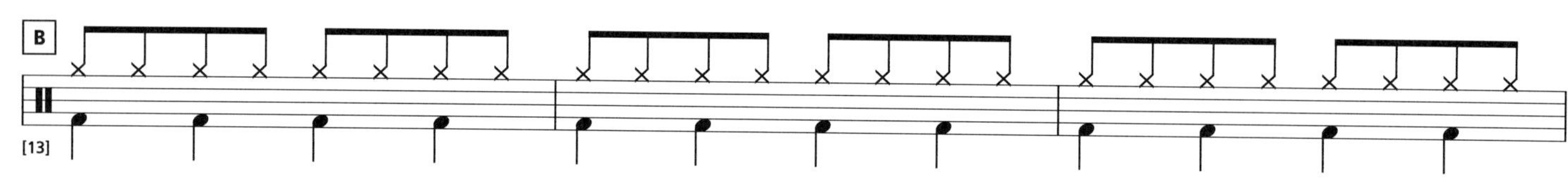

[16]
[19]
C
[21]
[24]
[27]
[30]

Walkthrough

A Section (Measures 1–12)

'Cuba Mama' opens with your hi-hat foot on the backbeat and continues with a rhythmic phrase played around the kit that leads into the mambo groove from measure 5.

Measure 1 | *Hi-hat foot*
Play your hi-hat foot on the backbeat in this measure. Aim to perform the movement with accuracy and conviction to avoid unnecessary splashing sounds. There are two techniques that can be used when attempting a hi-hat foot pattern: heel up and heel down. Use the technique that suits you best. With both techniques, ensure your foot always remains in contact with the hi-hat pedal.

Measures 3–4 | *Co-ordinating with the left foot*
The hands pattern in these measures follows the other instruments that play on the track. The rhythm is: 1 2 rest & rest & (measure 3) rest & 2 & 3 & 4 (measure 4). Try playing the fill on the snare only initially then, when the rhythms are clear, move it around the kit as written. Your hi-hat foot should continue to play on each backbeat throughout these measures. This might be quite challenging to co-ordinate accurately, but because there is nothing to play on the bass drum you can focus fully on the hi-hat and fill (Fig. 1).

Measure 5 | *Mambo*
This mambo beat consists of quarter notes on the ride cymbal, bass drum on beats 1 and 3, snare on beat 2 and varied toms. Maintain your right hand on the ride cymbal and aim to achieve even and consistent strokes. Play the snare and toms part with your left hand. Move it in good time and maintain a solid pulse. Co-ordinate this hand pattern with the bass drum and you are ready to mambo.

B Section (Measures 13–20)

The first four measures of this section are the build-up for the trumpet solo in measure 17. The section between measures 17 and 20 is marked with a repeat sign and should be played twice.

Measure 13–16 | *Build-up*
The drums play consistent quarter note bass drums and eighth note hi-hat until the fill in measure 16. It is common in Latin music for build-up sections such as this to feature two or more different rhythmic patterns played by the musicians. In this piece, the piano and bass play syncopated rhythms that might be confusing at first. However, the shaker plays a straight pattern that you can sync to. This is your chance to work on developing a stronger inner pulse.

Measure 17 | *Four-way co-ordination*
When playing the mambo beat in this section, you will need to add your hi-hat foot on the backbeat. This means you will use four limbs to play different patterns. This will be harder to do than co-ordinating only three. When practising four-way co-ordination it is common to take out and re-introduce the patterns until the full groove feels comfortable to play and is, more importantly, stable. Playing hi-hat foot with the backbeat snare is an important technique that can be used in many advanced grooves and various styles (Fig. 2).

C Section (Measures 21–31)

This section has a mambo beat similar to the A section but with a few added ride cymbals. The ending phrase is based on the introduction phrase in measures 3–4.

Measures 21–27 | *Sound production: ride cymbal*
In order to produce the best sound from the ride cymbal, allow your hand to bounce back after hitting the cymbal and ensure that your grip of the stick is not too tight. To achieve a clear ring from the ride, try playing with the tip of your drum stick and hitting the cymbal in the area half way between the bell and the edge of the cymbal. As with the drums, hitting the same area of a cymbal will naturally produce a more consistent sound.

Measure 31 | *Rhythmic displacement*
The ending fill consists of two groups of three snare strokes. The first group starts on the beat, and the second on the offbeat. Moving phrases across beats and measures is the basic concept of rhythmic displacement.

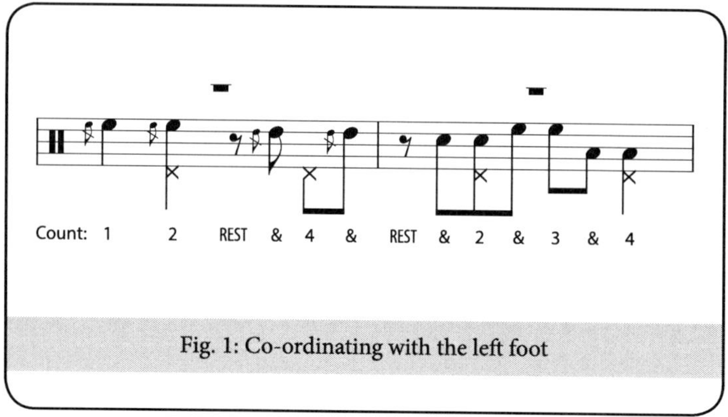

Fig. 1: Co-ordinating with the left foot

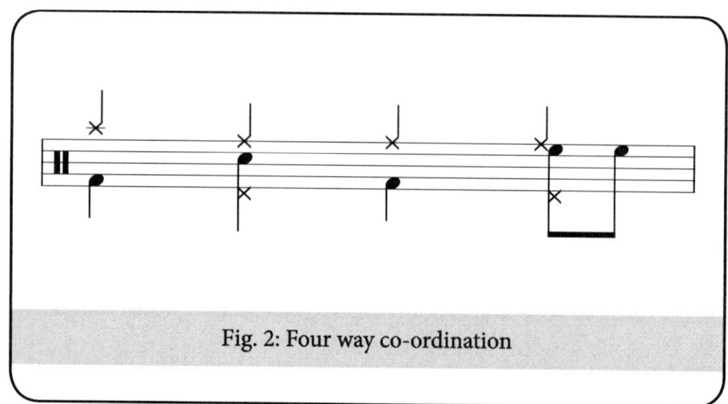

Fig. 2: Four way co-ordination

For You

SONG TITLE: FOR YOU
GENRE: R'N'B
TEMPO: 110 BPM

TECH FEATURES: BASS DRUM/SNARE UNISON
16TH-NOTE HI-HATS
SNARE FLAM

COMPOSER: NEEL DHORAJIWALA

PERSONNEL: NEEL DHORAJIWALA (PROD)
NOAM LEDERMAN (DRUMS)

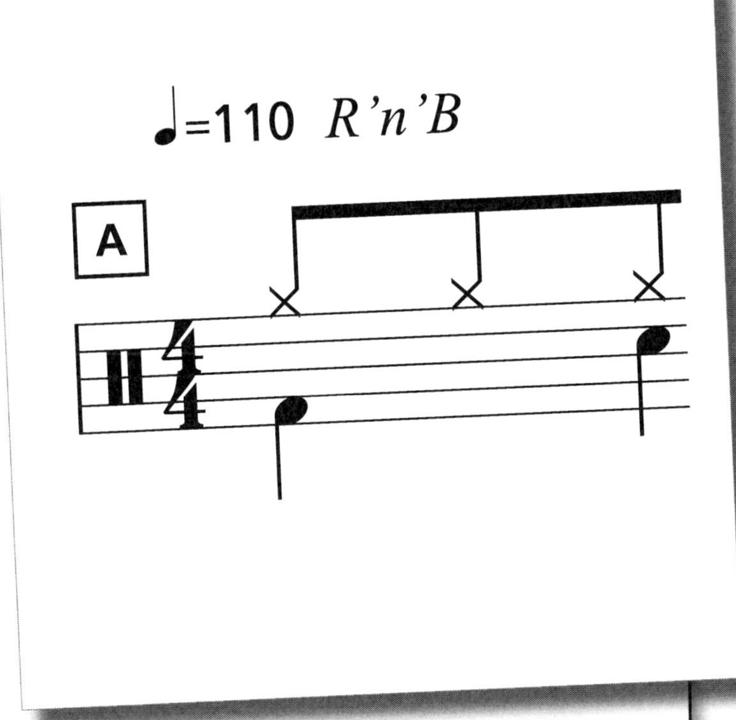

OVERVIEW

'For You' is a contemporary R'n'B, pop and hip hop influenced track produced in the style of artists like Ne-Yo and Usher. This genre is typified by programmed drum parts, electronic influenced instrumentation and a rich vocal arrangement coupled with a slick, polished production sound.

STYLE FOCUS

Contemporary R'n'B lends itself to programmed drum machine grooves. Deep electronic bass drums coupled with heavily compressed hand-claps over snare drums are typical. In this piece, hand claps on beats 2 and 4 lock into the groove while the bass drum pattern on the down beats provides a solid feel. Recorded drum parts are often interpreted for live performances and some who do this well include Aaron Spears, Gerald Heyward and Nisan Stewart. Many drummers in R'n'B have played gospel, which has no doubt influenced their feel and chops.

THE BIGGER PICTURE

The original term R&B stands for rhythm and blues, but R'n'B is a different genre. The last three decades have seen a remarkable evolution and development in the sound. For example, the 1980s sound of New Jack Swing, the early 1990s hip hop influence, the late 1990s neo soul movement and the polished sound of the 2000s all contributed to its transformation. Through taking all of these elements and interpreting them using modern production techniques and electronic instrumentation, the R'n'B sound continues to enjoy incredible commercial success, popularity and the scope to evolve.

RECOMMENDED LISTENING

There are many artists and producers to listen to in order to gain a better understanding of R'n'B. Studio productions worth checking out include Ne-Yo's *In My Own Words* (2006), *Because Of You* (2007) and *Year Of The Gentleman* (2008), Usher's *Confessions* (2004), Maxwell's *Maxwell's Urban Hang Suite* (1996), and Brandy's *Never Say Never (1998).*

It is just as important to listen to the live interpretations of the songs as it is to the studio produced versions. Drummer Aaron Spears is an awesome force on the live scene and his solo performance of Usher's *Caught Up* at the Modern Drummer Festival 2006 is a masterclass in contemporary R'n'B drumming.

For You

Neel Dhorajiwala

C
[17]

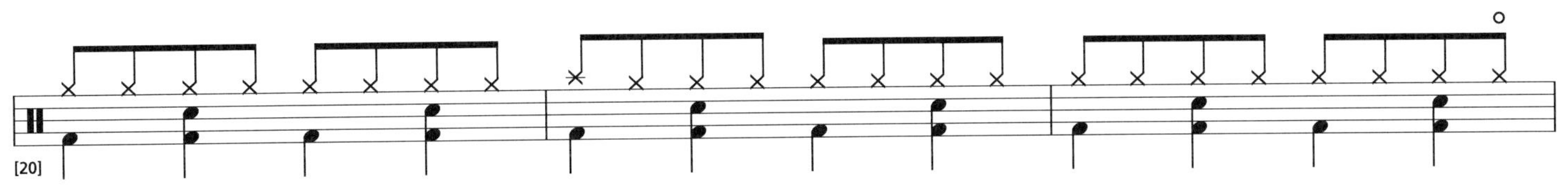
[20]

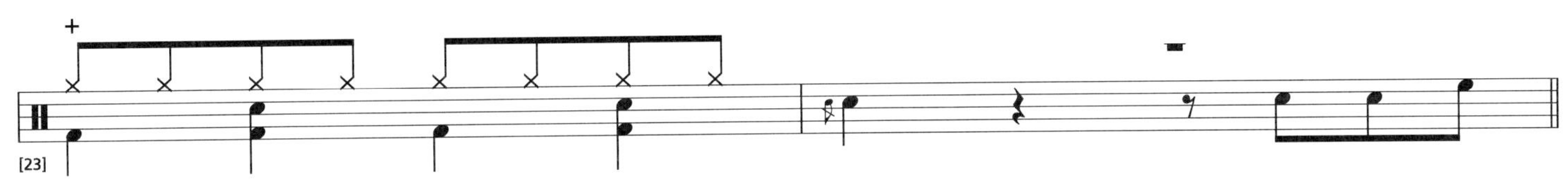
[23]

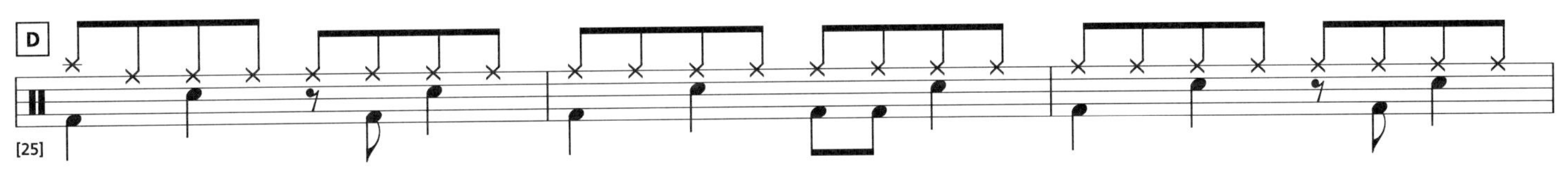
D
[25]

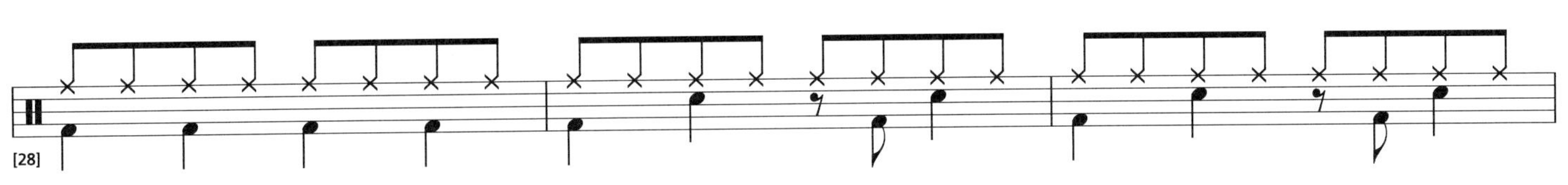
[28]

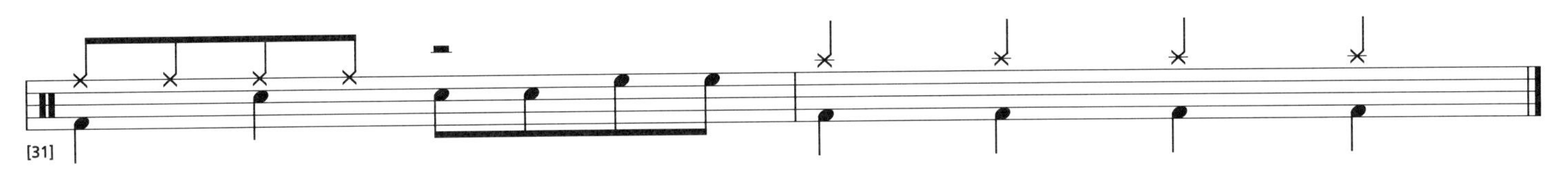
[31]

Walkthrough

A Section (Measures 1–8)

The first section of 'For You' showcases a basic hip hop beat with open hi-hats and bass drum variations.

Measure 2 | *Open hi-hat*
The 'o' sign above the hi-hat note means that it should be played in the open position. This open hi-hat sound is created by loosening the hi-hat pedal and hitting the hi-hat at the same time. In order to play in time you will need to co-ordinate the movement of your hi-hat foot with your hand that plays the hi-hat. Your hi-hat foot should stay in contact with the pedal because removing it will affect your posture, balance and timing. Avoid leaning backwards, sideways or forwards while performing this technique.

Measure 3 | *Closed hi-hat*
The '+' sign above the first hi-hat note in this measure indicates that the hi-hat should be played in the closed position. This is achieved by pressing the hi-hat pedal down with your foot and tightening the hi-hat cymbals. As with the open hi-hat, you still need to hit the hi-hat with your hand at the same time. This movement must be timed well or else the closed hi-hat will still sound like an open (or half open) hi-hat.

B Section (Measures 9–16)

Measures 9–16 | *Snare and bass variations*
The pattern introduced in section A continues to develop and vary throughout the B section. Try practising the snare and bass pattern without the cymbals and check that all of the rhythmic values are accurate. When you feel ready, add the cymbals and play along with the track or a metronome.

Measure 9 | *Sixteenth notes on the hi-hat*
Co-ordinate two 16th-note hi-hats with the groove in this section. This can be played with your right hand but it might be challenging because of the relatively fast tempo. It will be easier to move your left hand from the snare to the hi-hat in order to play the last 16th note of beat 2. You can continue to play consistent eighth notes on the hi-hat with your right hand, helping you to maintain a steady pulse (Fig. 1).

Measure 16 | *Crash hits*
In this measure there are four quarter-note crash beats to be played together with the bass drum. Ensure these are co-ordinated accurately and placed exactly on the beats. Hitting the crash with too much force might choke the sound of the cymbal so aim to hit it with balance.

C Section (Measures 17–24)

In this section, there is a groove somewhere between hip hop and dance music where the bass drum plays on every beat. The section ends with a flam on the snare followed by a fill.

Measures 17–23 | *Backbeat unison with bass drum*
In these measures the hi-hat, snare and bass drum should be played together on the backbeat. Co-ordinate your three limbs accurately and avoid any unnecessary flams as these will affect the flow of the groove. Playing a backbeat unison groove with the bass drum is an essential skill in a drummer's repertoire.

Measure 24 | *Fill*
This fill starts with a snare flam on beat 1, followed by a break until the '&' of beat 3 where the lead-in fill to section D begins. Count the beats between the break and the fill to play this measure accurately. Decide whether you want to reach the crash in measure 25 with your right or left hand and adjust the sticking on the fill in measure 24 accordingly (Fig. 2).

D Section (Measures 25–32)

The bass drum and snare patterns here are similar to the B section but your right hand plays on the ride cymbal.

Measure 32 | *Sound production: crash cymbal*
In order to produce the best sound from the crash cymbal, allow your hand to bounce back after hitting the cymbal and make sure that your grip of the stick is not too tight. To achieve a convincing sound from the crash, try playing with the neck part of your drum stick.

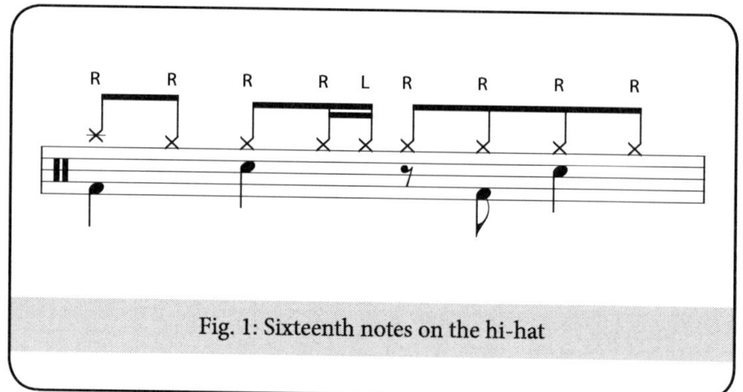

Fig. 1: Sixteenth notes on the hi-hat

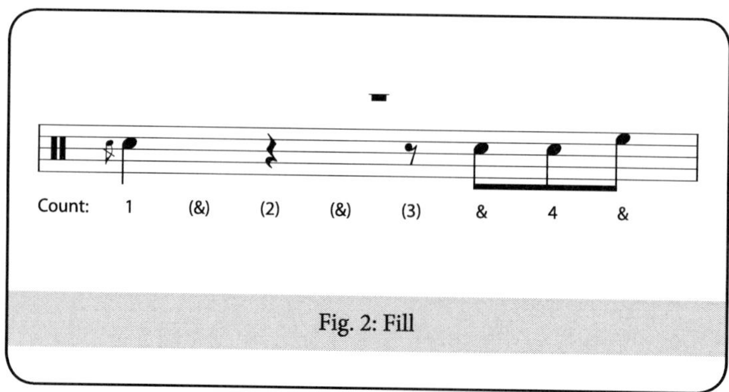

Fig. 2: Fill

SONG TITLE: SLIPSTREAM
GENRE: GRUNGE
TEMPO: 115 BPM

TECH FEATURES: POWER DRUMMING
SYNCOPATION
FLAMS

COMPOSER: JASON BOWLD

PERSONNEL: JASON BOWLD (ALL PARTS)

OVERVIEW

'Slipstream' is a grunge track inspired by bands like Nirvana, Pearl Jam and Alice In Chains. It features flams, syncopation, a ride groove and power drumming among its techniques.

STYLE FOCUS

Grunge drumming is essentially about being honest with your sound. Fills are limited to flams, cymbal and tom accents should be played only to complement the song. This is especially the case with 'Slipstream'. As usual, solid timing and consistency with your power are vital in keeping the energy flowing in the music. Focusing on keeping the audio mix of the bass drum, snare, toms and cymbals well-balanced will improve your sound and serve the music well.

THE BIGGER PICTURE

The term grunge was coined by Mark Arm, singer of the Seattle band Mudhoney (known as the godfathers of grunge) back in the early 1980s. This hybrid of punk, rock and indie spawned hundreds of bands who set themselves apart from the mainstream rock of the decade, most notably Melvins, Pixies and Sonic Youth. In the late 1980s, Alice In Chains and Soundgarden introduced elements of classic rock and metal to the grunge mix.

In the early 1990s, Nirvana and Pearl Jam achieved mainstream success. Nirvana's *Nevermind* (1991) topped the US charts, becoming one of the 100 best-selling albums of all time thanks to 'Smells Like Teen Spirit', the video for which was played repeatedly by MTV. The irony of its success was not lost on frontman Kurt Cobain, who abandoned *Nevermind*'s glossy production on their follow-up *In Utero* (1993).

RECOMMENDED LISTENING

A good place to start with grunge is with the bands Mudhoney and Pixies. Tracks such as 'Pump It Up' and 'Touch Me I'm Sick' by Mudhoney, and 'Wave Of Mutilation' by Pixies exemplify grunge drums. The albums *Bleach* (1989), *Nevermind* and *In Utero* by Nirvana feature Dave Grohl on drums, who epitomises the genre's style with his powerful flam accents, memorable drum fills and jumpy, understated beats. Pearl Jam's albums carry a more sophisticated edge. Early tracks 'Jeremy' and 'Even Flow' from their debut *Ten* (1991) highlight the talent of their first drummer Dave Krusen.

Slipstream

Jason Bowld

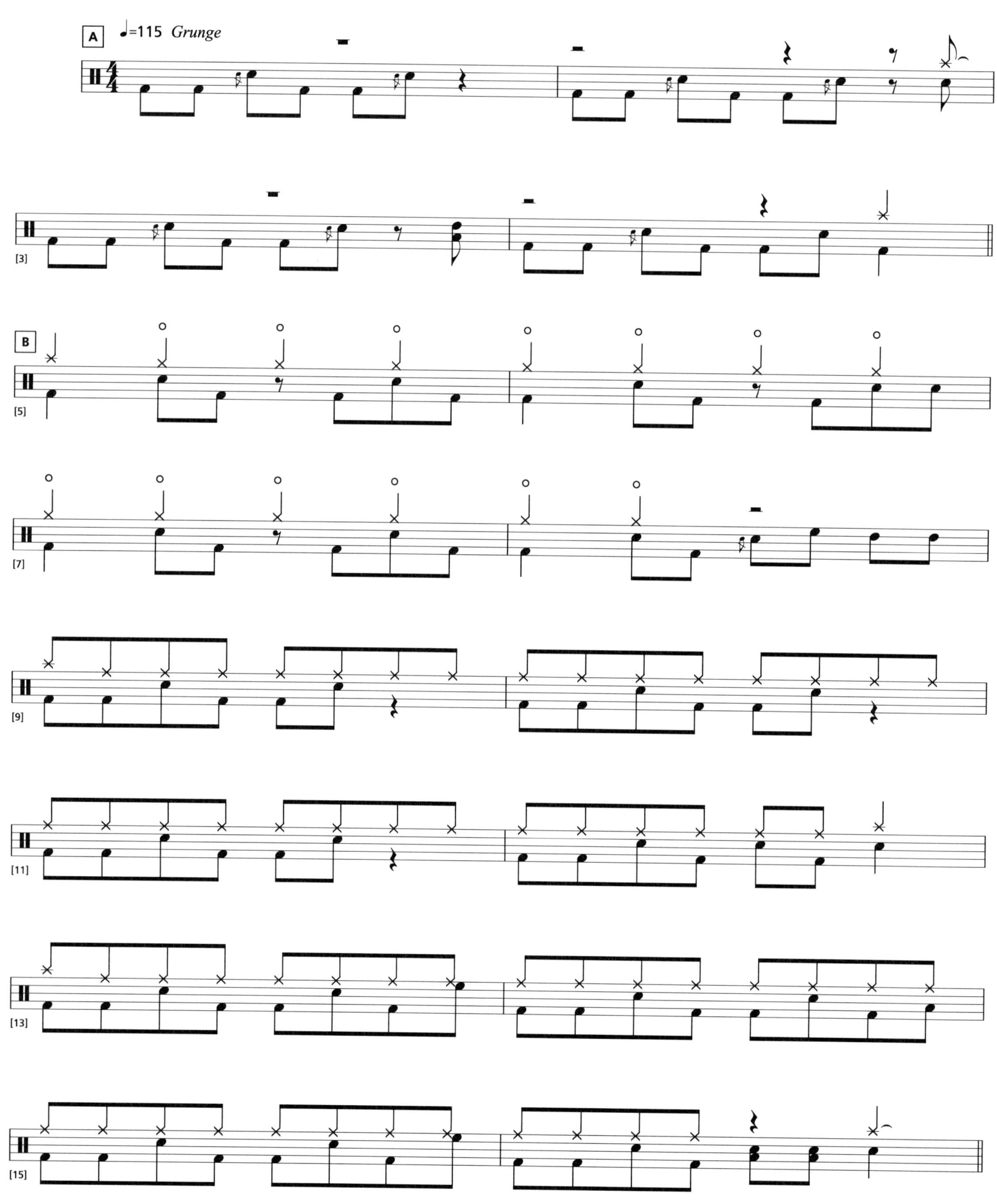

C

[17]

[19]

[21]

D

[23]

[25]

[27]

[29]

[31]

Walkthrough

A Section (Measures 1–4)

The song's verse is split into two sections, A and B. The A section consists of a broken version of the chorus groove played in measures 9–16 and is characterised by the space left at the end of each measure.

Measures 1 | *Flam groove*
The main groove here focuses on playing flams on beat 2 and the offbeat of beat 3.

Measures 2–3 | *Counting during the flam groove*
In measures 2 and 3 there are hits on the offbeat of beat 4 played on the snare and crash, then the two toms. To remain aware of the space between beats, count during these measures.

Measure 4 | *Setting up the B section*
A single snare is played here before the crash on beat 4. This mirrors the guitar riff and sets up the B section.

B Section (Measures 5–16)

This section's steady rock groove locks in with the music.

Measures 5–7 | *Rock groove*
The groove contains quarter notes played on the open hi-hat. Counting will help you keep time because the groove is quite slow, which means there is more chance of error. The rhythm for the main groove in measure 5 is 1, 2&3&4& (Fig. 1).

Measure 8 | *Eighth-note fill*
The groove concludes with an eighth-note fill which starts on beat 3 with a snare flam then travels around the toms.

Measures 9–12 | *Ride groove*
The ride plays steady eighth notes with the bass and snare that drop out on beat 4, except in measure 12 where a snare and crash are played on this beat.

Measures 13–15 | *Busier ride groove*
The ride groove develops as the bass and snare play through the measures without stopping. A tom is also added on the offbeat of beat 4. For a more consistent sound, try not to accent the ride when you play the snare and toms. You can achieve this by using small arm movements to play the ride.

Measure 16 | *Ride groove fill*
The fill played in this groove on beat 3 sets up the C section. When you come off the floor tom, go for a crash that is within easy reach of your right hand.

C Section (Measures 17–22)

This long build-up starts with staccato type hits on the snare and toms, moving to an eighth-note flow with floor tom, snare and bass.

Measures 17–18 | *Stabs*
These challenging stabs measures will require preparation. Start by working on the rhythms in each measure as follows. Measure 17: '1 2 3 & rest &'. Measure 18: '1 & 2 & 3 & 4'. Next, play the two-measure phrase on the snare only and use a metronome to ensure the pulse remains consistent. The next step will be to incorporate the notated drum voices. Ensure you take your time to play them accurately and in unison. Lastly, add the flams on the snare and the final crash hit in measure 18 (Fig. 2).

Measures 19–22 | *Tom groove*
In this tom groove, your right hand stays on the floor tom with your left hand and bass drum sharing the flow of eighth notes. Measure 22 begins without the floor tom but with snare and cymbal accents and ends with a flam on beat 4. Place the main flam stroke on the beat and the grace note just before it.

D Section (Measures 23–32)

This final section is essentially a reprise of the B section.

Measures 23–26 | *Rock groove*
This is the same as measures 5–8. Use Fig. 1 to count the rhythm.

Measures 27–32 | *Ride groove*
There is a reprise of the ride groove that you played in measures 13–16 in the last six measures of the piece. After the fill in measure 30 on beat 3, remember to hold for three beats in measure 31 and to play the final fill as '4& 1'.

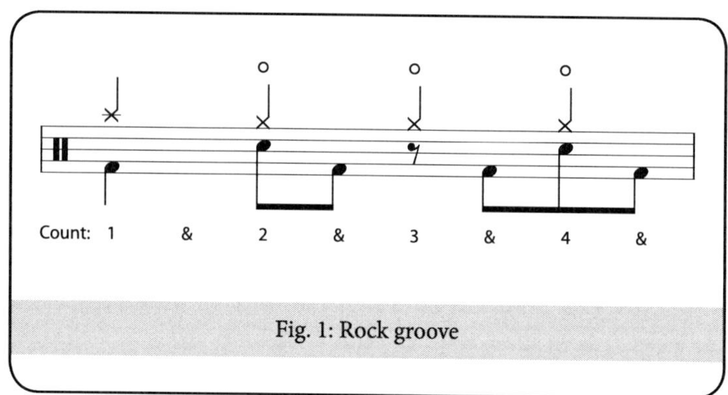

Fig. 1: Rock groove

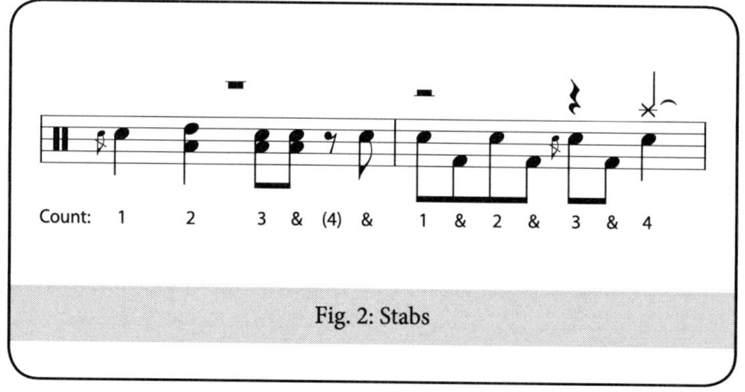

Fig. 2: Stabs

SONG TITLE: Y'ALL
GENRE: POP/ALTERNATIVE
TEMPO: 102 BPM

TECH FEATURES: OPEN HI-HAT
SYNCOPATION
FLAMS

COMPOSER: HENRY THOMAS

PERSONNEL: NOAM LEDERMAN (DRUMS)
HENRY THOMAS (BASS & PROD)
NEEL DHORAJIWALA (PROD)

OVERVIEW

'Y'All' is a pop/alternative track in the style of Beck, NERD and Gorillaz, all of whom have been influenced by alternative hip hop. It features open hi-hat, syncopation and flams among its techniques.

STYLE FOCUS

Typically of alternative hip hop tracks, the drumming on 'Y'All' could just as easily be the work of a machine as a human being. Alternative hip hop usually relies on samples as well as live musicianship. Your time keeping needs to be as steady as a metronome because if you start speeding up or slowing down the samples will be out of time with the beat and you risk pulling the track apart.

THE BIGGER PICTURE

Alternative hip hop was a reaction to the prevalence of gangsta rap in the 1990s. Artists like Digable Planets, Arrested Development and A Tribe Called Quest rejected the negative tone of gangsta rap, instead embracing Afrocentric lifestyles and absorbing elements from other genres including the musical motifs of blues and reggae.

Alternative hip hop has not enjoyed the same commercial success as gangsta rap. However, the genre's eclecticism has continued to influence household acts from Outkast to Beck. Between them, these last two artists alone have combined blues, folk, rap and funk.

The British group Gorillaz are a recent example of alternative hip hop's potential to cross musical boundaries and produce new, exhilarating styles. Their sound encompasses samples, hip hop, pop and rock, often all at once. They also use programmed beats that have a strong hip hop flavour.

Many alternative hip hop acts perform with live musicians. The Roots are a good example of this and their drummer Ahmir 'Questlove' Thompson has incredibly steady hands, making it often impossible to distinguish his beats from those of a drum machine.

RECOMMENDED LISTENING

'Loser' from Beck's album *Mellow Gold* (1994) is an example of alternative hip hop and 'Devil's Haircut' from *Odelay* (1996) is worth investigating. Gorillaz' 'Dare' is their own take on disco, while 'Dirty Harry' has a funky, syncopated groove and 'Clint Eastwood', a stripped back pattern that will test your timekeeping.

Y'All

Henry Thomas

♩=102 *Pop/Alternative*

A

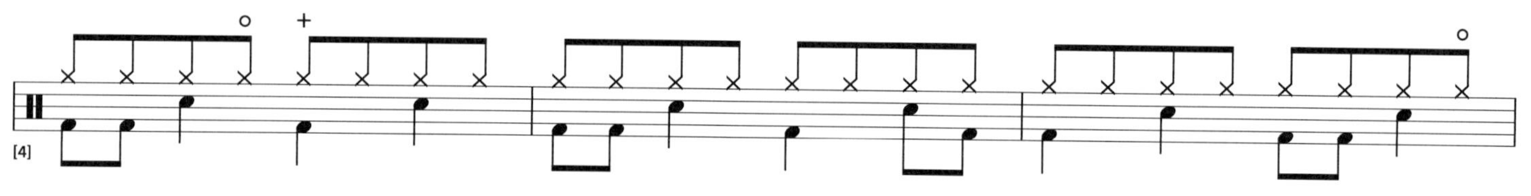

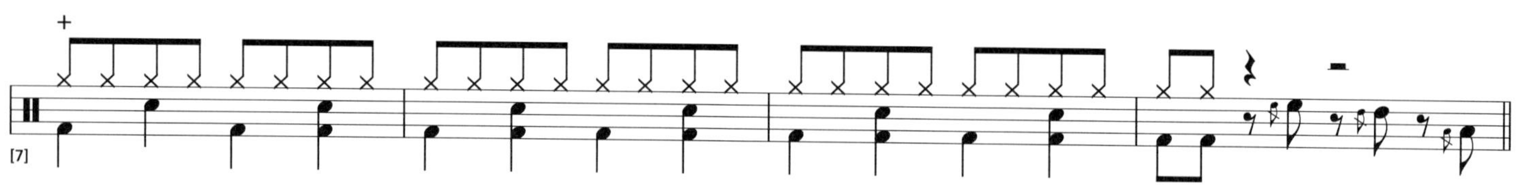

B

[11]

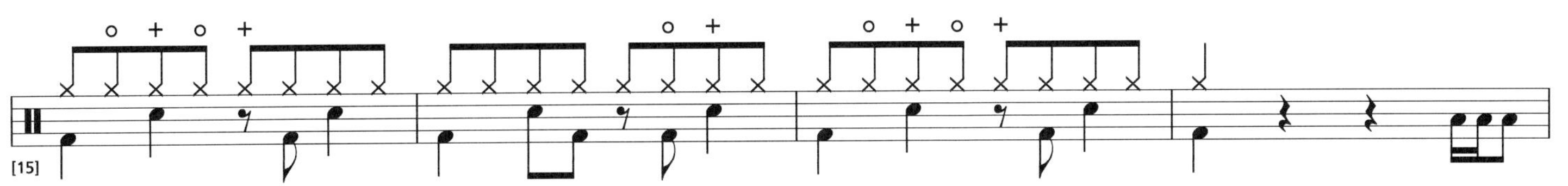
[15]

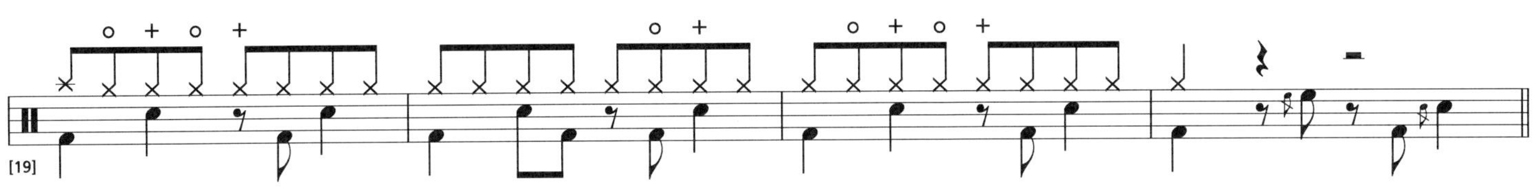
[19]

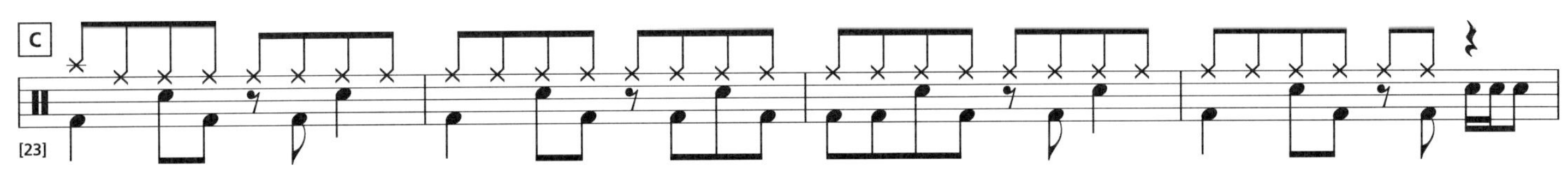
C
[23]

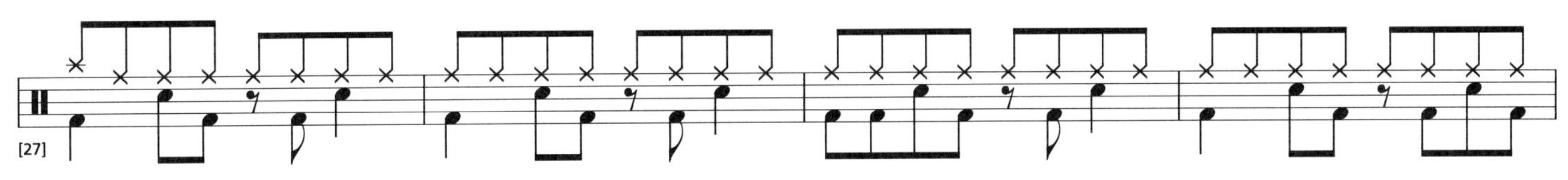
[27]

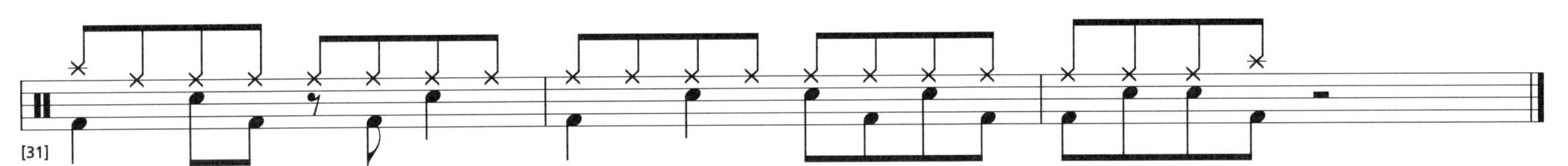
[31]

Walkthrough

A Section (Measures 1–10)

The first section features a few drum beats that are common in this style of drumming. There is also a fill in measure 10 that introduces offbeat flams on the toms.

Measures 1–9 | *Changing grooves*
In measures 1 and 2 there is an introduction groove without a full backbeat pattern. However, from measure 3 all backbeat snares are included. In measures 7–9, a unison groove with bass drum on every quarter note is present. Moving between grooves smoothly is a challenge, so practise each measure separately.

Measure 8 | *Backbeat unison with bass drum*
Play the hi-hat, snare and bass drum together on the backbeat. Co-ordinate your three limbs accurately and avoid any unnecessary flams that will affect the flow of the groove.

Measure 10 | *Offbeat flams on toms*
Following the two eighth notes on beat 1, there are three offbeat flams played on the high, medium and floor toms. Use the appropriate flam technique and aim to place the main stroke that follows the grace note of the flam exactly on the offbeats. During the eighth-note rests, move both hands and prepare for the next stroke (Fig. 1).

B Section (Measures 11–22)

The groove develops here with snare and bass drum variations as well as open hi-hats on the offbeats.

Measure 11 | *Open hi-hat*
In this measure, there is a groove with two open and two closed hi-hats. Perform these techniques accurately and in sync with the backing track. Set your hi-hat pedal in the most comfortable position to help you perform this well (Fig. 2).

Measure 18 | *Break and fill*
There is a quarter note bass drum with a hi-hat on the first beat of this measure followed by two quarter-beat rests on beats 2 and 3, and a fill on beat 4. Counting the beats between the break and fill will ensure continuity and a stronger sense of pulse. On beat 4, there is a rhythmic phrase that consists of two 16th notes and an eighth note. This should be counted as "4 e &".

C Section (Measures 23–33)

The groove moves to the ride cymbal in this section and you will see a few more bass drum variations and crashes.

Measures 23–33 | *Snare and bass variations*
The pattern introduced in section B continues to develop and vary throughout the section. Try practising the snare and bass pattern without the cymbals and ensure that all of the rhythmic values are accurate. When you feel ready, add the cymbals and play along with the track or a metronome.

Measures 23–33 | *Sound production: cymbals*
You will produce the best sound from the cymbals by allowing your hand to bounce back after hitting the cymbal, and ensuring that your grip of the stick is not too tight. These principles, along with well timed hand-foot co-ordination, will help you to produce clear open and closed hi-hat sounds. For a convincing sound from the crash cymbal, play with the neck part of your drum stick and use the tip for the ride cymbal.

Measure 26 | *Snare fill*
The fill in this measure is played on the fourth beat and follows the same rhythmic phrase that was used in measure 18. The most straightforward way to perform this would be to have both of your hands on the snare, using the following sticking: R L R. Your right hand should move from the ride cymbal to the snare but maintain a consistent eighth-note pattern so that your focus can be on playing the second 16th note with your left hand accurately.

Measure 33 | *Ending phrase*
This consists of four eighth notes followed by a two beat rest. In the top part of the stave there are three consecutive ride cymbals followed by a crash. The first eighth note in the bottom part of the stave is played with the bass drum followed by two snare hits and another bass drum stroke in sync with the crash. Practise each part separately then put them together and work on accurate co-ordination.

Fig. 1: Offbeat flams on toms

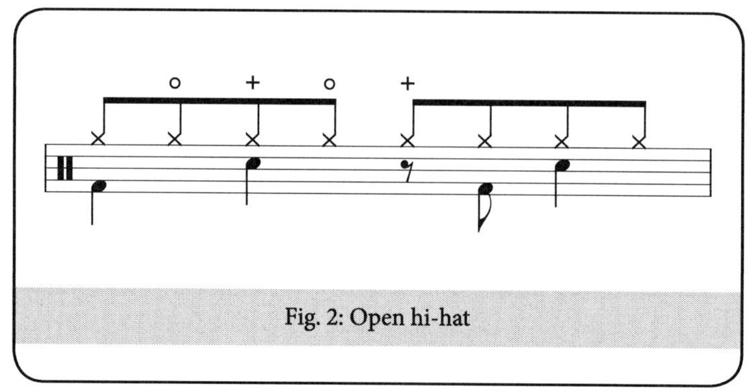

Fig. 2: Open hi-hat

Technical Exercises

In this section the assessor will ask you to play a selection of exercises drawn from each of the four groups shown below. In addition there is a Fill exercise which you will play using the designated backing track. You do not need to memorise the exercises (and can use the book in the assessment) but the assessor will be looking for the speed of your response.

The stickings shown (L & R) are there as a guide for right handed drummers. Left handed drummers should reverse the sticking patterns. Before you start the section you will be asked whether you would like to play the exercises along with the click or hear a single measure of click before you commence the test. Groups A–D should be played at ♩= 70.

Group A: Single and Double Strokes

Single and double strokes in eighth and 16th notes, alternate measures

Group B: Paradiddles

Single paradiddle in 16th notes with accents

Group C: Flams

Flams in quarter notes

Group D: Triplets

Triplets in eighth notes with alternate stickings

Group E: Fill

In the assessment you will be asked to play the three measure groove shown followed by one of the notated fills chosen by the assessor. The fills consist of alternating eighth- and 16th-note single and double strokes, and flams. You will perform this exercise to the backing track. The tempo is ♩= 70.

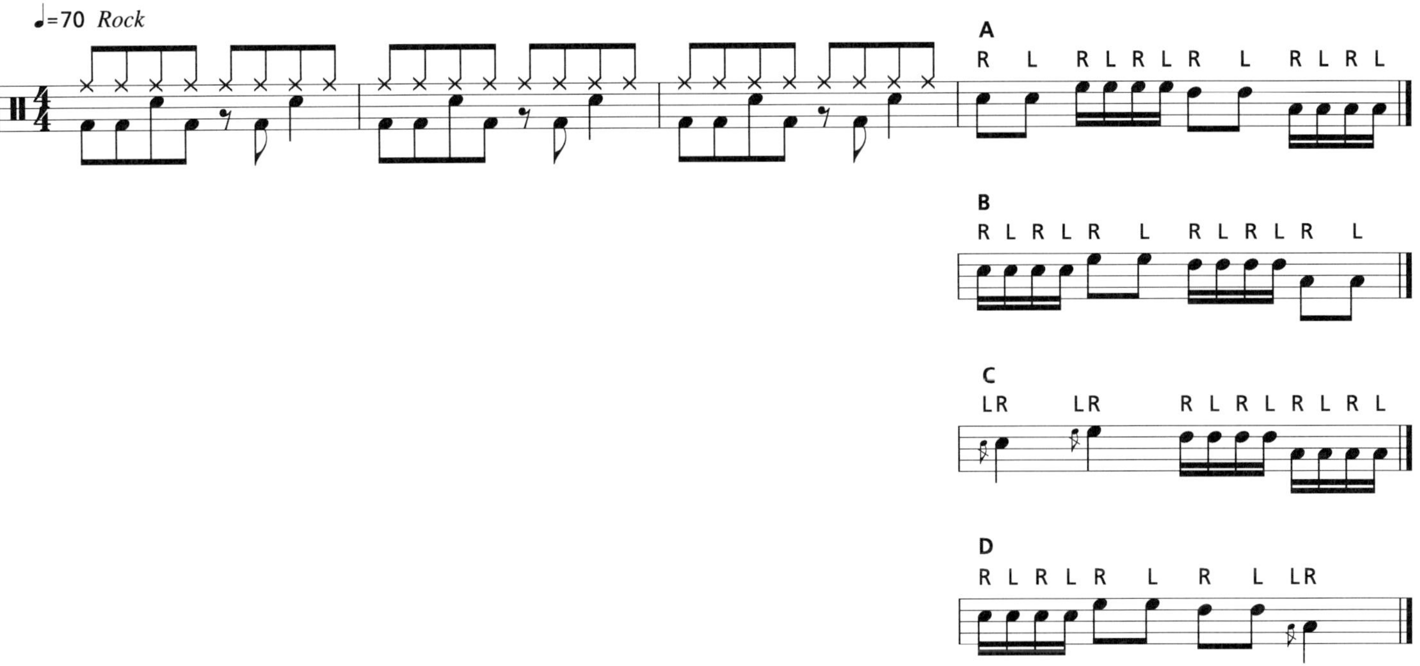

Sight Reading

In this section you have a choice between either a Sight Reading test or an Improvisation & Interpretation test (see facing page). You will be asked to prepare a Sight Reading test which will be given to you by the assessor. The test is four measures long and played on the snare drum. The assessor will allow you 90 seconds to prepare it and will set the tempo for you. The tempo is ♩= 70.

Improvisation & Interpretation

You will be asked to play a written one-measure groove, vary it in the following two measures and improvise a fill in the fourth measure. The test will be played to a backing track using the bass drum, hi-hat and snare drum. You have 30 seconds to prepare then you will be allowed to practise during the first playing of the backing track, before playing it to the assessor on the second playing of the backing track. This test is continuous with a one-measure count-in at the beginning and after the practice session. The tempo is ♩= 80.

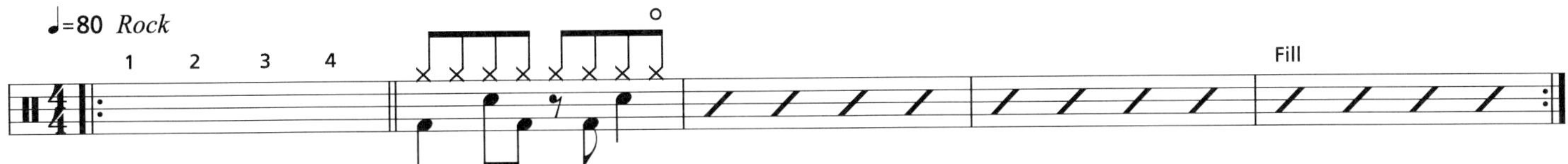

Ear Tests

There are two Ear Tests in this level/grade. The assessor will play each test to you twice. You will find one example of each type of test printed below.

Test 1: Fill Playback and Recognition

The assessor will play you a one-measure fill in common time played on the snare drum. You will play back the fill on the snare drum. You will then identify the fill from two printed examples shown to you by the assessor. You will hear the test twice.

Each time the test is played it is preceded by a one-measure count in. There will be a short gap for you to practise. Next you will hear the vocal count in and you will then play the fill to the click. The tempo is ♩=70.

Test 2: Groove Recall

The assessor will play you a two-measure groove played on the bass drum, hi-hat (open and closed) and snare. This is a two-measure groove that is repeated. You will hear the test twice. You will be asked to play the groove back on the drum voices indicated for four measures.

Each time the test is played it is preceded by a one-measure vocal count-in. The tempo is ♩=80.

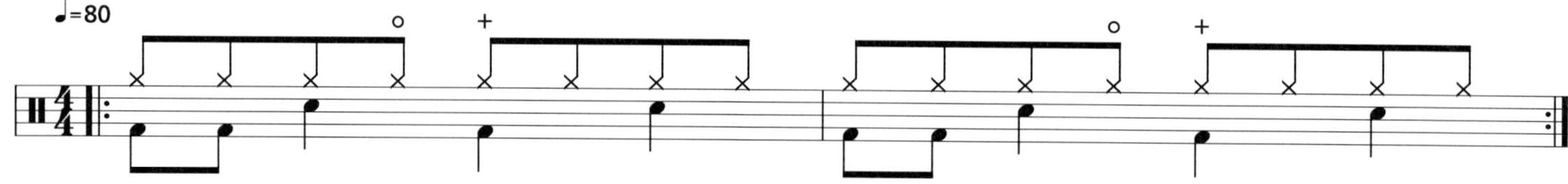

General Musicianship Questions

In this part of the assessment you will be asked five questions. Four of these questions will be about general music knowledge and the fifth question asked will be about your instrument.

Music Knowledge

The assessor will ask you four music knowledge questions based on a piece of music that you have played in the assessment. You will nominate the piece of music about which the questions will be asked.

In Level/Grade 2, you will be asked:

- Drum voices on the stave
- The meaning of time signature marking
- Quarter, dotted eighth note, eighth note and 16th note values
- Rest values
- Repeat markings including first and second time measures

Instrument Knowledge

The assessor will also ask you one question regarding your instrument.

In Level/Grade 2 you will be asked to identify:

- The following parts of the drum kit – bass drum, snare, high tom, medium tom, floor tom, hi-hat, ride cymbal and crash cymbal
- The following parts of the drumstick – tip, neck, shaft and butt
- Two main drum kit makes

Further Information

Tips on how to approach this part of this assessment can be found in the *Syllabus Guide* for Drums, the Rockschool *Drums Companion Guide* and on the Rockschool website: *www.rslawards.com*.

Entering Rockschool Assessments

Entering a Rockschool assessment is easy, just go online and follow our simple six step process. All details for entering online, dates, fees, regulations and Free Choice pieces can be found at *www.rslawards.com*

- All candidates should ensure they bring their own Level/Grade syllabus book to the assessment or have proof of digital purchase ready to show the assessor.

- All Level/Grade 6–8 candidates must ensure that they bring valid photo ID to their assessment.

Marking Schemes

Debut to Level/Grade 5 *

ELEMENT	PASS	MERIT	DISTINCTION
Performance Piece 1	12–14 out of 20	15–17 out of 20	18+ out of 20
Performance Piece 2	12–14 out of 20	15–17 out of 20	18+ out of 20
Performance Piece 3	12–14 out of 20	15–17 out of 20	18+ out of 20
Technical Exercises	9–10 out of 15	11–12 out of 15	13+ out of 15
Sight Reading *or* Improvisation & Interpretation	6 out of 10	7–8 out of 10	9+ out of 10
Ear Tests	6 out of 10	7–8 out of 10	9+ out of 10
General Musicianship Questions	3 out of 5	4 out of 5	5 out of 5
TOTAL MARKS	**60%+**	**74%+**	**90%+**

Levels/Grades 6–8

ELEMENT	PASS	MERIT	DISTINCTION
Performance Piece 1	12–14 out of 20	15–17 out of 20	18+ out of 20
Performance Piece 2	12–14 out of 20	15–17 out of 20	18+ out of 20
Performance Piece 3	12–14 out of 20	15–17 out of 20	18+ out of 20
Technical Exercises	9–10 out of 15	11–12 out of 15	13+ out of 15
Quick Study Piece	6 out of 10	7–8 out of 10	9+ out of 10
Ear Tests	6 out of 10	7–8 out of 10	9+ out of 10
General Musicianship Questions	3 out of 5	4 out of 5	5 out of 5
TOTAL MARKS	**60%+**	**74%+**	**90%+**

Performance Certificates | Debut to Level/Grade 8 *

ELEMENT	PASS	MERIT	DISTINCTION
Performance Piece 1	12–14 out of 20	15–17 out of 20	18+ out of 20
Performance Piece 2	12–14 out of 20	15–17 out of 20	18+ out of 20
Performance Piece 3	12–14 out of 20	15–17 out of 20	18+ out of 20
Performance Piece 4	12–14 out of 20	15–17 out of 20	18+ out of 20
Performance Piece 5	12–14 out of 20	15–17 out of 20	18+ out of 20
TOTAL MARKS	**60%+**	**75%+**	**90%+**

* Note that there are no Debut Vocal assessments.

Drums Notation Explained

BASS DRUM & TOMS

Bass drum | Floor tom | Medium tom | High tom

SNARE

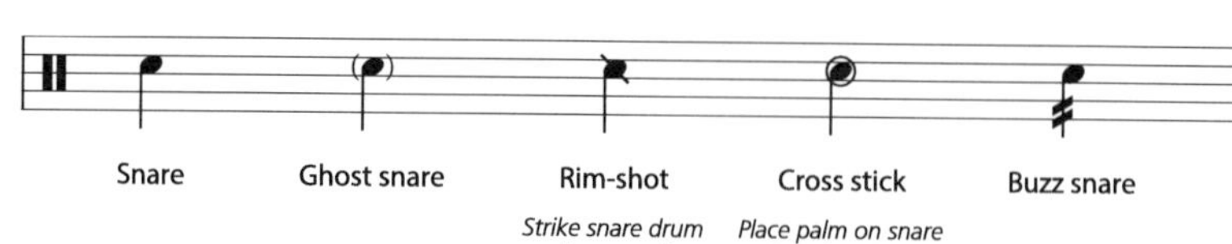

Snare | Ghost snare | Rim-shot | Cross stick | Buzz snare

Rim-shot: *Strike snare drum and surrounding rim at same time*

Cross stick: *Place palm on snare drum head and strike rim with stick*

HI-HAT

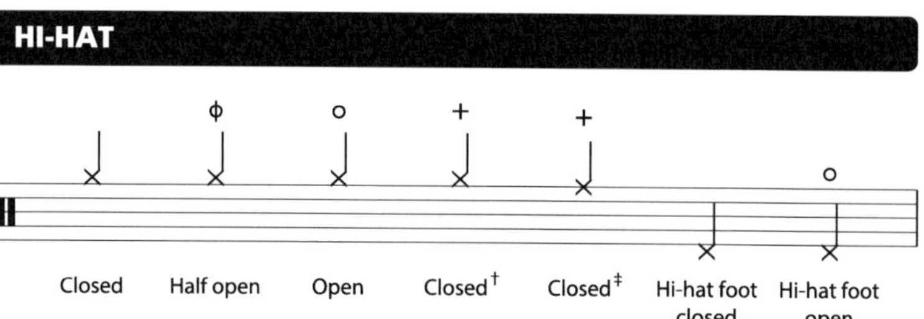

Closed | Half open | Open | Closed† | Closed‡ | Hi-hat foot closed | Hi-hat foot open

† Used on the first closed hi-hat that follows an open hi-hat

‡ The hi-hat is closed without being struck. Note that the hi-hat closed (cross) symbol may appear above drum voices other than the hi-hat (as shown above). This simply means another drum voice is being played at the same moment that the hi-hat is being closed.

OTHER CYMBALS

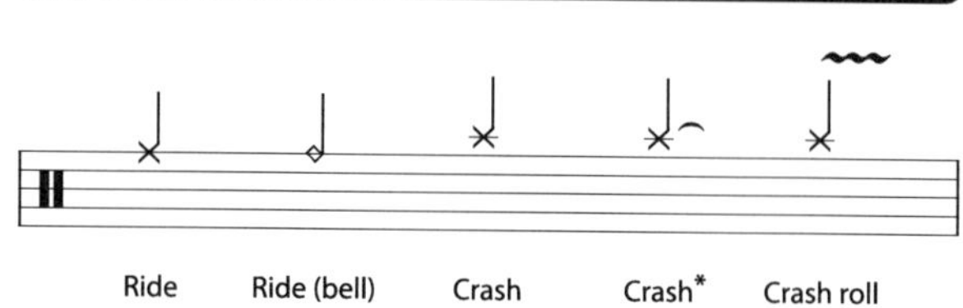

Ride | Ride (bell) | Crash | Crash* | Crash roll

***Allow all cymbals to ring on** unless explicitly stopped, as indicated by the keyword **'Choke'**. Occasionally ties may be used (*) to emphasise that cymbals should be allowed to ring on. This can avoid confusion during syncopations and pushes.*

GENERAL MUSIC NOTATION

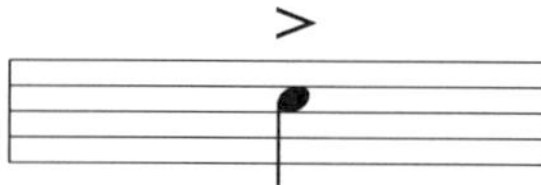

Accentuate note (play it louder).

Slashes are used to demarcate measures during solos, fills, developments and other ad lib. sections.

D.𝄋. al Coda

Go back to the sign (𝄋) then play until the measure marked ***To Coda* 𝄌** then skip to the section marked **𝄌 *Coda***.

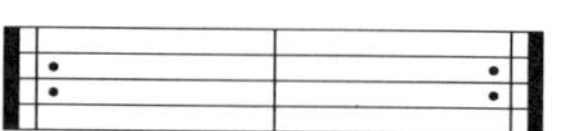

Repeat the measures between the repeat signs.

D.C. al Fine

Go back to beginning of song and play until the measure marked ***Fine*** (end).

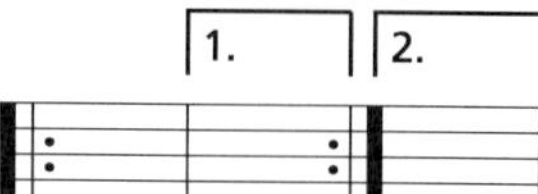

When a repeated section has different endings, play the first ending only the first time and the second ending only the second time.

Repeat the previous measure. In higher levels/grades these may also be marked *sim.* or *cont. sim.*

Repeat the previous two measures. In higher levels/grades these may also be marked *sim.* or *cont. sim.*

In rudiments, each stem slash subdivides the note value by half.

MUSICAL TERMS WITH SPECIFIC EXAMINATION DEFINITIONS

Fill	Play an individual, stylistic fill.
Cont. sim.	Continue in similar way but vary the pattern slightly.
Develop	Extend the musical part in a stylistically appropriate manner.
Rit. (ritardando)	Gradually slow the tempo.

Mechanical Copyright Information

Losing My Religion
(Buck/Mills/Stipe/Berry)
Universal/MCA Music Limited

I Heard It Through The Grapevine
(Whitfield/Strong)
EMI Music Publishing Limited.

Passion Fruit
(Shebib/Rogues/Graham)
EMI Music Publishing Limited/Kobalt Music Publishing Limited

Maggie May
(Stewart/Quittenton)
Warner/Chappell Music Limited/EMI Music Publishing Limited

Georgia On My Mind
(Gorrell/Carmichael)
Chester Music Limited trading as Campbell Connelly & Company

Relegation Riddim
(Davies/Broderick)
Sony/ATV Music Publishing/Downtown Music UK Limited

mcps